Getting Beyond "I Like the Book"

Creating Space for Critical Literacy in K–6 Classrooms

Vivian Vasquez

With

Michael R. Muise

Susan C. Adamson

Lee Heffernan

David Chiola-Nakai

Janice Shear

INTERNATIONAL Reading Association

800 Barksdale Road, PO Box 8139
Newark, Delaware 19714-8139, USA
www.reading.org

Director of Publications   Joan M. Irwin
Editorial Director, Books and Special Projects   Matthew W. Baker
Production Editor   Shannon Benner
Permissions Editor   Janet S. Parrack
Acquisitions and Communications Coordinator   Corinne M. Mooney
Associate Editor, Books and Special Projects   Sara J. Murphy
Assistant Editor   Charlene M. Nichols
Administrative Assistant   Michele Jester
Senior Editorial Assistant   Tyanna L. Collins
Production Department Manager   Iona Sauscermen
Supervisor, Electronic Publishing   Anette Schütz
Senior Electronic Publishing Specialist   Cheryl J. Strum
Electronic Publishing Specialist   R. Lynn Harrison
Proofreader   Elizabeth C. Hunt

Project Editor   Charlene M. Nichols

Cover   Design, Linda Steere; Photo, Vickie Vasquez

Library of Congress Cataloging-in-Publication Data
Vasquez, Vivian Maria.
  Getting beyond "I like the book" : creating space for critical literacy in K–6 classrooms / Vivian Vasquez with Michael R. Muise … [et al.].
      p. cm. — (Kids InSight series)
Includes bibliographical references and index.
  ISBN 0-87207-512-5
  1. Language arts (Elementary)--Social aspects--United States. 2. Literacy--Social Aspects--United States. 3. Multicultural education--United Staets. 4. Critical pedagogy--United States. 5. Children--Books and reading--United States. I. Title. II. Series.
  LB1576.V37 H87 2003
  371.1--dc21

                                                                      2003004933

Contents

Note From the Series Editor

It is a pleasure to introduce readers to Vivian Vasquez; her colleagues Michael R. Muise, Susan C. Adamson, Lee Heffernan, David Chiola-Nakai, and Janice Shear; and the kindergarten, third-, fifth, and sixth-grade students featured in *Getting Beyond "I Like the Book": Creating Space for Critical Literacy in K–6 Classrooms*. In this book, Vivian and her collaborators describe the literacy activities that occur in six different classrooms. Throughout the book, we are provided the opportunity to look closely at how these outstanding teachers and their students use children's books and other texts to engage in important discussions in which young people learn the skills needed to be able to read, but also learn to critically analyze the texts they are reading and consider how to use what they learn to improve their own and others' lives. I am pleased that Vivian, Mike, Susan, Lee, David, and Janice's book has been selected by a respected panel of literacy experts to be published in the Kids InSight (KI) Series; I believe their book makes an outstanding contribution to the field of elementary-level students' literacy development.

The KI series provides practical information for K–12 teachers and brings to the fore the voices of and stories about children and adolescents as the basis for instructional decisions. Books in the series are designed to encourage educators to address the challenge of meeting the literacy needs of all students as individuals and learners in and out of our classrooms, while recognizing that there are no easy answers or quick fixes for achieving this goal. Sociocultural perspectives of how students learn are the foundation of each KI book, and authors address learners' emotional, affective, and cognitive development. Strategies and actions embraced by teachers described in KI books include the following:

- dialoguing with other professionals;
- reading research findings in literacy and education;
- inquiring into teaching and learning processes;
- observing, talking with, and listening to students;
- documenting successful practices; and
- reflecting on literacy events using writing and analysis.

Authors of these books allow us to see into classrooms or view students' lives outside school to learn about the thoughts and dreams of young people, as well as the goals and planning processes of teachers. Finally, we are privy to how events actually unfold during formal and informal lessons—the successful and the less-than-successful moments—through the use of transcripts and interview comments woven throughout KI books.

In this book, the authors show us how to keep kids *in sight* as they bring us into conversations that learners have around various texts, including books, posters, letters, and journals. For example, kindergartners help us understand why they became concerned when they didn't see women portrayed as Mounties in a Royal Canadian Mounted Police poster hanging in their classroom. Listening to their voices, we see them analyze whether the women were left out of the picture because they couldn't ride horses, and thus couldn't be in the police force, or if another reason existed. Vivian, their teacher, led them to further challenge traditional notions of femininity and masculinity. The children decided to research the topic at the library. Through posing questions, the students read various texts closely, discovering that the poster had a notation indicating that this picture depicted an all-male police force. These kindergartners moved beyond the discussion of the poster to thinking about the jobs women and men assume, reading books about women in various jobs, and thinking about what they could do to help change some negative ways that women and girls are viewed in some societies. This full circle of activities designed to foster higher-level thinking shows the power of critical literacy—that it is more than reading the words on the page and more than responding to a good book or text—it is questioning and critiquing. And it is seeking to make change in society based on new learnings. These are the types of learners we want to develop in democratic societies.

Vivian, Mike, Susan, Lee, David, and Janice also help us glean insights as we examine the strategies teachers employ to address tensions that arise during literacy practices. For example, Lee used books with her third graders that prompted them to bring up issues that were difficult to understand and often uncomfortable to talk about. Some of these books focused on issues of racism and equity. Lee developed strategies to guide these discussions, often starting by reading the book aloud and allowing students to "linger" over the story for several days. The gift of time allowed students to feel safe in their responses and talk about issues because they had a chance to hear others and think about formulating their responses. Lee shares a six-session flexible guide for us to try out with our learners to facilitate these kinds of thoughtful conversations.

In another chapter, Susan and Janice share ways that teachers can use process drama to respond to reading literature. This strategy helps students develop reasonable ways to solve struggles they may be having in school or in the community, such as racism. In examining the drama talk, we see students work out various ways to respond to problems—from unworkable to reasoned solutions—and we understand why students need to get the silly/unworkable responses out and be coached toward reasonable solutions. Process drama also can be used to help students engage in critical literacy—students addressing issues of power and how power affects who learns, who has the freedom to play outside safely, and other issues of social justice.

In another chapter of the book, Mike shares strategies he used with his fifth- and sixth-grade students when they chose to go to Canada's Wonderland Amusement Park for their end-of-year trip and he realized that school rules might prevent such an excursion. To convince the principal and superintendent that they should be allowed to go on the trip of their choice, the students engaged in many math activities related to events at the park. They also sought to make a case for the educational and entertainment value of the trip and sent persuasive letters to administrators. Although they were unsuccessful in their efforts, the students learned a great deal about critiquing school practices and developing reasoned techniques for helping others see their point of view.

Finally, David and his sixth-grade students help us see the many texts in the media that learners encounter daily (e.g., Nike logo) and how they require critique. He offers us the strategy that we cannot just promote critique of what is wrong or not working in our society or in the texts we read, but we must help students think about how to act based on their critiques. Social action is how we change our world into a better place for everyone.

Throughout *Getting Beyond "I Like the Book": Creating Space for Critical Literacy in K–6 Classrooms*, Vivian and her colleagues help readers grapple with teaching and learning issues by urging us to write responses to questions posed, gather data from our classrooms, reflect upon what we see, and generate new possibilities for what could be. These authors help us understand how teachers must be willing to help students see their worlds differently and take action based on careful critique—with actions based on the desire to make change for the good of oneself and others. I cannot think of a more worthy educational goal.

Deborah R. Dillon
Series Editor
University of Minnesota, Twin Cities
Minneapolis, Minnesota, USA

Kids InSight Review Board

Jan Turbill
University of Wollongong
Wollongong, New South Wales,
    Australia

Angela Ward
University of Saskatchewan
Saskatoon, Saskatchewan,
    Canada

Deborah A. Wooten
University of Tennessee
Knoxville, Tennessee, USA

Josephine P. Young
Arizona State University
Tempe, Arizona, USA

Acknowledgments

I would like to thank each of my collaborators in this project for sharing significant moments in their lives as teachers and learners. Their insight and willingness to negotiate spaces for critical literacies in various contexts using different texts are an inspiration to us all. On behalf of my coauthors, a sincere thank-you goes out to our families, friends, and colleagues for their support when much of our time was consumed with writing. Our gratitude also goes out to our students and their families who have made our work both challenging and pleasurable.

In the book, I talk about common denominators and what brought the authors of this book together. One such denominator was Jerry Harste, who has always had a way of building community. In part, this book came into being because of his encouragement to read more, write more, and think together. This book was also written with esteemed colleagues in mind, specifically Andy Manning, Barbara Comber, Allan Luke, and Hilary Janks.

Deborah Dillon, you recognized the potential for this book and made it easy for my collaborators and me to grow it into the publication that it is today. Thank you for your sensitivity and support. You have a delicate touch that was much appreciated! Matt Baker, your efficiency and constant support came at just the right time. Thank you for traveling to Washington, D.C., to iron out details and meet publication deadlines. You helped to make the process enjoyable. Charlene Nichols, you were such an important part of this project. You took the stress out of the final moments in the publication process. Joan Irwin, from the first time we met you have encouraged and supported my work—thank you.

Finally, a special thank-you to Andy Bilodeau, who has never wavered in his support of my multiple projects. Your patience, "go for it" attitude, and editorial and technical help make it easier for me to fill the blank page.

VV

Chapter 1

Setting the Context: A Critical Take on Using Books in the Classroom

Patricia:	*Are you sure you looked?*
Alexandro:	*Everywhere in there!*
Patricia:	*She [the librarian] even helped me. She said, "I guess we don't have any."*
Alexandro:	*Did you tell her that's not fair?*

It was November. My kindergarten students and I (Vivian Vasquez) had been together for three months and had gotten to know one another quite well. During this time I had attempted to construct a curriculum and make use of pedagogy to create opportunities for us to dialogue about diversity using the varied linguistic and cultural experiences and resources that this ethnically diverse group of children brought to the classroom.

The brief conversation between Patricia and Alexandro took place one day after returning from a visit to our school library. They had been looking for a book on the Philippines as one way to support Emma, a new student in the class, whose family had just moved to Canada from the Philippines. Their quest was met with frustration when they learned there were no books with characters who might be Filipino, nor were there any resource books on the Philippines. In a sense these children were learning about the notion of being "other," of not having spaces and opportunities to belong. Patricia and Alexandro's frustration led me to suggest a class project focusing on the question, Do we see ourselves in books that are in our school library? A topic such as this may seem too difficult or complex for young children. For some children this may be true, however, from the beginning of the school year my students had available to them more powerful ways of talking about the world as I framed my teaching from a critical literacy perspective. This is also true for the other students and teachers you will meet in this book. The critical literacy perspective I speak of here is similar to the perspective suggested by Flint and Riordan-Karlsson (2001) in their Kids InSight book *Buried Treasures in the Classroom: Using Hidden Influences to Enhance Literacy Teaching and Learning*—to encourage conversation related to social issues. Barbara Comber's definition of critical literacy is applicable. She states that critical literacies include practicing the use of language in powerful ways to get things done in the world, to enhance everyday life in schools and communities, and to question practices of privilege and injustice (Comber, 2001). Critical literacy is also about imagining thoughtful ways of thinking about reconstructing and redesigning texts and images to convey different, more socially just and equitable messages that have real-life effects in the world.

The project was an important one that raised questions of moral responsibility and the role that our class could play in negotiating new, more equitable social spaces.

Our school was pre-K to eighth grade with approximately 800 students. It was located in a middle income neighborhood in a suburb of Toronto, Ontario, Canada. In our class of 18 students, we had 11 different ethnicities represented including children from Malta and Peru. The children and I were therefore disturbed when we searched through the shelves of our school library over the next few weeks and discovered

- there were no books on the Philippines,
- the books on Peru were outdated and were published in the 1970s, and
- there were no books on Malta.

Earlier in the school year, I talked to the children about acting on issues that were of concern to us; that is, doing something about problems we face in the school community and beyond in order to contribute to building more democratic ways of being and doing at our school. At that time we made a list of possible types of actions including finding out as much as we could about an issue in order to discuss and analyze it in a critical way.

We talked about writing letters, doing research to find more information on a topic, and asking to meet with individuals involved to make our concerns public. We also looked at our own ways of doing and saying things and how we may have contributed to existing problems by not acting on them.

To address our concern regarding the lack of culturally diverse books in our school library, we engaged in a conversation regarding possible solutions. One suggestion made by a group of children was to write a letter to the librarian (see Figure 1). The letter makes public the findings of the students' discoveries in the library. Along with the letter, we attached a list of books with characters from diverse ethnicities and backgrounds and bilingual books that could be purchased for our school library. This list was created by one of the boys in the class together with his parents.

**Figure 1
Letter to the Librarian**

From Vasquez, V. (2000). Building community through social action. *School Talk, 5*(4), p. 2.

The librarian was very receptive to the letter. When presented with the findings, she appeared genuinely disturbed. Like many people, she had not thought about the marginalization of certain individuals and groups of students when they are unable to "see themselves" in books and other texts used in school. She immediately worked on ordering books to address our concerns. She also began rethinking the decisions she made regarding which books to display based on who is represented and not represented by those books.

As part of our project, we created a newsletter outlining the work that we had done. This newsletter was taken home by students and was one way of filtering our class inquiry into some of the children's homes. From the newsletter, Mena and her family began to explore how different cultures are represented by the way in which books are displayed at local bookstores. She and her parents talked to the manager of their neighborhood bookstore, emphasizing the need for books that represent diverse cultures to be available all year, not just for special events such as Black History Month or Women's History Month. Anthony and his mother questioned why children's literature was hidden away in the back corner of their local bookstore, and why a computer to locate books was not available in the children's section as it was in other areas of the store. It was amazing to learn about ways that my students had taken what they had learned in the classroom into their homes to engage in projects with their parents.

Reflection Point 1.1 _____

This first Reflection Point is deliberately lengthier than the others in this book. The questions that follow are meant to provide a contextual basis for reading the remainder of the book.

1. Obtain a journal in which to write any thoughts, comments, connections, or questions as you read this book. Begin by reflecting on your own experience as a young learner. What kinds of books do you recall reading while you were an elementary school student? In what ways did the books that were made

available to you reflect your own experiences? In what ways were the books that were made available to you inconsistent with your own experiences? What were some of the ways that you talked about these books? What purpose did they serve in your life?

2. Make a list of all the children in your classroom, noting their cultural backgrounds. Then walk around the classroom paying close attention to the children's available literature. Write about how closely the books in your classroom reflect the cultural makeup of your students.

3. Together with your students, make a list of books that you feel should be added to your classroom or school library to ensure that all the children in the class are reflected in the books available to them. It would be very useful to add to this list throughout the school year.

How This Book Was Conceptualized

This book began from a common interest among a group of educators to find ways of bringing a critical dimension to existing classroom curriculum and from an interest in children and books written for children. It represents a collaboration among educators who are connected with life in elementary school classrooms. I, Vivian Vasquez, am the common denominator for each of the other five collaborators of this book. I met each of them through study groups or graduate school courses. My voice (Vivian) dominates this chapter along with chapter 2 and chapter 6 more so than in the others primarily because I was the one who proposed writing about our collective experiences with critical literacy and books. From here on "I" will refer to me, and "we" will refer to the thoughts of my collaborators and me as a group. The third person is used when referring to the work done by one of my five collaborators, and italics are used to indicate personal thoughts from each.

I am currently an assistant professor at the School of Education at American University where I work closely with classroom teachers and preschool- and elementary school-age children. However, previous to this I was a preschool and elementary school teacher for 14 years who explored ways of making curriculum critical. Susan C. Adamson is the program director at Indiana Partnership for Young Writers. Lee Heffernan is a doctoral candidate at Indiana University, Bloomington, as well as a public school teacher. Michael R. Muise is a former elementary school teacher and is now an assistant professor at Wayne State University. Susan, Lee, and Mike have been exploring notions of critical literacy for at least five years. David Chiola-Nakai is a teacher librarian in an elementary school in Canada. He was introduced to critical literacy while taking a master's course more than six years ago. Also represented in this book is work done by Janice Shear, a veteran elementary school teacher, also from Canada.

This book represents the varied experiences of my collaborators and me as we attempted to move our students' responses to text beyond the traditional "I like the book" by putting a critical edge on kindergarten to sixth-grade students' talk about books and other texts. It is not about literature study per se but about using books differently in combination with other texts to create spaces for critical literacy. It consists of detailed critical literacy events and instances from our classrooms, as well as practical classroom strategies and annotated lists of children's literature that can be used as one source to encourage and support critical conversations. The names of colleagues and students that appear in this volume are pseudonyms.

Even though we each worked with children of different ages and, at the time this book was conceived, had different experiences with critical literacy, we learned from one another and used one another's experiences as a way of pushing our own teaching practices. Those of us who worked with younger children drew from the work done by those of us who worked with older children. We adopted and adapted one another's teaching practices to best support our individual teaching contexts. In each of our settings we did not worry so much about leveling books but considered what sorts of work we could accomplish with a particular book or part of a book. This is based on our shared belief that what is deemed inappropriate for one child may be perfectly appropriate for another. We see this as a matter of knowing our students and the cultural capital they bring to the classroom. Bourdieu (1991) refers to cultural capital as cultural or social ways of being or doing that are objectified or embodied in the individual as a type of habitus or as a sort of publicly recognized credential.

My collaborators and I hope that our stories intersect with experiences you have had and that they lead you to consider engaging in critical literacies in your context.

Using Critical Literacies to Get Things Done in the World

In the opening vignette, we entered my (Vivian's) kindergarten classroom where Patricia and Alexandro led the charge for changing the kinds of books that were made available in the school library. As they engaged in this act, they helped to break the pattern of privileging some students (those students who find themselves in books) while marginalizing others (those students, like Emma, whose experiences are not represented in the books available in the school library).

In a selective review of literature, Comber (1992) identified three different principles that guide approaches to critical literacy. She found that in classrooms where a critical literacy position is advocated, teachers

- Reposition students as researchers of language.

  To do this, students are given opportunities to understand and learn how language works in the world by engaging in analysis such as discussing how different combinations of words convey different kinds of messages.

- Respect student resistance and explore minority culture constructions of literacy and language.

  To do this, teachers provide space in the curriculum to address the diverse needs of students, including ensuring the curriculum speaks to the cultural ways of being of the class members and the varied discourses (experiences with literacy, literate ways of being, and language use) that those students bring to the classroom.

- Problematize classroom and public texts.

  To do this, teachers help students to interrupt and analyze texts that are often considered natural or neutral. For example, students and teachers together look closely at the illustrations and choice of words used in texts such as books and magazine advertisements.

One of the ways that my collaborators and I initiated the children we worked with into a socially critical approach to literacy was by problematizing classroom and public texts and by repositioning students as researchers of language. It is our work using literature in combination with other texts to introduce critical conversations in our classrooms and to construct social action projects that is the focus of this book. Specifically, the ways we used books on four particular fronts will be presented.

1. Pairing Everyday Texts With Texts Written for Children

   Everyday texts are real-world texts that can be found as part of daily living. These include news clips, advertisement fliers, posters, greeting cards, and other such items. In this book you will learn about ways that these texts can be paired with texts written for children as one way to begin to negotiate critical literacy in the classroom.

2. Focusing on Social Issues by Bringing the Outside World Into the Classroom

   Social issues are real-world issues that are important to children. Later in the book you will read about ways that classroom teachers have created spaces or opportunities for taking up these issues as part of the classroom curriculum.

3. Using Children's Literature to Unpack Social Issues in the School Community

   Books are one of many tools that can be used to create space to discuss social issues in the classroom. In the following chapters we will share some of the ways that classroom teachers have used books along with other texts as a starting point for taking up and analyzing such issues.

4. Using Children's Literature Critically in the Content Areas

   Often, critical literacy has been discussed, written about, and promoted as something to be done as part of the literacy curriculum.

Later in the book, Michael Muise will share his experience in beginning to consider the role that critical literacy can play in the math curriculum.

Each of chapters 2 through 5 focuses on one of these fronts. Common to all chapters, however, is the way that each of my collaborators and I, together with our students, used books in some way to create space for taking thoughtful social action. That is, in each chapter we demonstrate ways in which we worked with our students on changing or addressing particular inequities in each of our own settings. It is important to note that while working from one front it is possible, and in fact likely, that other fronts would also be addressed.

Children's Literature in Elementary School Settings

Children's literature has played a major role in elementary school classrooms for years. The widespread use of literature across the school curricula has created multiple opportunities for children and their teachers to interact with these literacy texts in a variety of ways, including critically reading books, as Patricia, Alexandro, and my other kindergarten students did when they raised concern regarding the absence of particular kinds of books in our school library.

Because this is a book that uses critical literacy as a framework for talking about teaching and learning, I am compelled, if only briefly, to take up the very term *children's literature* and the tensions it creates. "Unlike terms like 'children's art' or 'children's games,' which express a sense of ownership on the part of children, 'children's literature' does not" (Rudd, 1999, p. 40). Adults in the children's market write most of the books labeled *children's literature*. However, there are growing, but still limited, accounts of young people writing for other young people such as Benjamin Lebert's *Crazy* or Alejandro Gac-Artigas's *Yo Alejandro* (see Appendix A for examples of books written for young people by young people). For the purposes of this book, *children's literature* refers to books written for the children's market. I acknowledge that the term *children's literature* is not unproblematic; however, it is used here simply because it is a term most common to educators.

The take on critical literacy presented here is not about the books per se, but what is done using books in different contexts and in combination with other texts such as posters and advertisements, as well as the kinds of perspectives brought to bear on talk about books. It is about creating spaces or opportunities for looking at the ways texts and images are constructed and constructive; in other words, how books are produced and how books position readers in particular ways by conveying messages such as what boys can do versus what girls can do. It is about creating opportunities for critical conversations. Flint and Riordan-Karlsson refer to this work as making available different social positionings to students as they engage with texts: "Social position considers how peers perceive each other as members of the learning community and as viable partners for specific literacy events" (2001, p. 5). Texts refer to books and everyday print and media publications such as magazine articles, advertisement fliers, and television commercials. Further explanation of everyday texts appears later in this chapter and in chapter 2.

Working From a Theory of Language and Learning

The opening vignette offered a number of important insights into teaching and learning from a critical literacy perspective. When I asked Patricia and Alexandro why they felt it was important to have books on the Philippines or books that included characters that look Filipino, they offered two reasons. First, they said that having books on the Philippines was one way for them to learn about a country, and second, if there were no books with Filipino-looking characters, then it might be harder for Emma to "tell her stories." When asked to clarify what "telling her stories" meant, they explained, "That means that Emma can say like in my home or like when this happened to me or that happened to me or that's not what I think and if there's no books with Philippines people then it'll be hard to say that." They continued by suggesting, "it isn't fair that other people are in books and Emma isn't." In other words, Patricia and Alexandro recognized that books present different kinds of realities:

providing spaces for readers to connect their own experiences and understanding for purposes of reaffirming those experiences and understandings, or for taking issue with the realities that are presented for them. Further, they recognize that particular students' experiences and understandings are marginalized when they do not find themselves in books or when the realities presented do not represent their experiences.

Patricia and Alexandro are developing a critical perspective in the way that they use language to critique and in the way that they critique the language and images in books. How did they come to this perspective? In a sense, they have come to learn how to use language to critique in great part due to the critical discourses or analytical ways of being that have been made available to them in the classroom. The ways of being I refer to are similar to those used by the other teachers who collaborated with me on this book. Each of the six of us has worked to some degree within a framework similar to that proposed by Harste (2001) in his Halliday Plus Model of Language Learning (see Figure 2).

Halliday Plus Model of Language Learning

The Halliday Plus Model can be used as a framework to consider what kinds of literate beings we want our students to become in the world. It builds on what we already know about language, making use of what has worked and problematizing what hasn't worked. It is based on a belief that literacy is socially constructed, and that when different ways of being are made available, literacy can be reconstructed. It begs the questions, What discourses maintain certain social practices? For what purpose? and To whose advantage? It also builds on the notion of individuals being multiliterate—that there isn't just one literacy but different literacies that allow different access in a variety of contexts and spaces in the world. In a practical sense, this means that it is not enough for children to learn language, to learn about language, and to learn through language, but that children also need to learn to use language to critique (Harste, 2001). According to Harste,

> the ability to sound out words and make meaning from texts makes children good consumers rather than good citizens. To be truly literate, children need to understand how texts work and that they as literate beings have options in terms of how they are going to respond to a particular text in a given setting. (2001, p. 2)

Figure 2
Halliday Plus Model

Learning Language	Learning About Language
Using language and other sign systems as a meaning-making process.	Understanding how texts operate and how they are coded.
Examples of using language to learn. • Read-aloud • Shared reading • Partner reading • Readers Theatre • Independent reading and writing • Writer's notebook • Big Books • Journals • Reading logs	Examples of teaching practices that help students learn about language. • Teaching letter-sound relationships • Comprehension strategies • Minilessons • Demonstrations • Focused lessons • Class charts
Learning Through Language	Learning to Use Language to Critique
Using reading and writing as tools and toys for learning about the world.	Using language to question what seems normal and natural as well as to redesign and create alternate social worlds. • Social action projects
Examples of teaching practices that help children to learn through language. • Using text sets • Reflective journals • Literature study • Inquiry or focused study • Sketch to stretch • Process drama	• Building off everyday texts and social issues. • Using texts that provide opportunities for interrogating the word and the world.

From Harste, J.C. (2001). The Halliday Plus Model. In K. Egawa and J. Harste, Balancing the literacy curriculum: A new vision. *School Talk*, 7(1), p. 2.

Figure 3
Exploring Ways in Which Language Is Used in the Classroom

Things that I do to teach language.	Things that I do to teach about language.
Things that I do to help my students learn through language.	Things that I do to help children use language to critique.

*Reflection Point 1.2*_____

Use the chart in Figure 3 or re-create it in your journal to situate your own literacy teaching by noting in what ways you are using language in your classroom.

Luke and Freebody's Four Resources Model

As we reflected on and analyzed our observations, we made use of another theoretical tool, namely, Luke and Freebody's Four Resources Model (refer to *Reading Online* at http://www.readingonline.org/research/lukefree body.html for more information about the model). In the model, Luke and Freebody (1999) assert that literacy is never neutral, that literacy is always situated within a series of ideologies or beliefs that shape what we do. While developing their model, Luke and Freebody examined existing and proposed literacy curricula and pedagogical strategies. They state that effective literacy draws from a repertoire of practices that allow learners, as they engage in reading and writing activities, to participate in various "families of literate practices." Luke and Freebody use the term *practices* to denote work that is actually done by literate beings in classrooms and beyond as an indication that these are negotiated, carried out, and achieved in everyday contexts unlike terms such as *schemata* or *competencies*, which denote a more individual, psychological model of literacy. In the Four Resources Model, four dynamic and fluid "families of (social) practices" are described.

1. Code-Breaking Practices

   These practices refer to having access to the skills required to break the code of written texts by recognizing and using fundamental features and architecture, including alphabet, sounds in words, spelling, and structural conventions and patterns.

2. Practices That Provide Opportunities to Participate With Text

   These practices involve participating in understanding and composing meaningful written, visual, and spoken texts, taking into account each text's interior meaning systems in relation to a reader's available knowledge and experiences of other cultural discourses, texts, and meaning systems.

3. Practices for Using Text

   These practices involve using texts functionally by knowing about and acting on the different cultural and social functions that various texts perform inside and outside school, and understanding that these functions shape the way texts are structured, their tone, their degree of formality, and their sequence of components.

4. Practices That Create Space for the Critical Analysis of Text

These practices involve the critical analysis and transformation of texts by acting on knowledge that texts are not ideologically natural or neutral—that they represent particular points of views while silencing others and influence people's ideas—and that their designs and discourses can be critiqued and redesigned in novel and hybrid ways.

Each family of practices is needed for literacy learning, but none in isolation is sufficient. Each of the four is inclusive with each being integral to the achievement of the others.

In the 1970s and 1980s, psycholinguistic and schema theory emphasized reader-text interactions, drawing attention to "text-meaning practices" or, more specifically, the construction of a reader who used textual and personal resources to coproduce a meaningful reading. In the late 1980s and early 1990s, sociolinguistic and sociosemiotic theory focused attention on language in use during which reading was viewed in terms of what it did, or could accomplish, pragmatically in the real world.

Currently, Luke and Freebody assert that reading should be seen as a nonneutral form of cultural practice, one that positions readers in advantageous and disadvantageous ways. They argue that readers need to be able to interrogate the assumptions and ideologies that are embedded in text as well as the assumptions that they, as sociocultural beings, bring to the text. This leads to asking questions such as, Whose voice is heard? Who is silenced? Whose reality is presented? Whose reality is ignored? Who is advantaged? Who is disadvantaged? These sorts of questions open spaces for analyzing the discourses or ways of being that maintain certain social practices over others.

Reflection Point 1.3_____

In your journal, reflect on your current theory of language and learning. How does what you do in the classroom reflect what you believe?

Rethinking Balanced Literacy

While using any model of literacy such as the Halliday Plus Model or Luke and Freebody's Four Resources Model, described previously, it is easy to fall into the trap of using such a model to balance a literacy program by doing equal amounts of everything or doing a little of this and a little of that. Rather, what we propose is for you to use such models as frameworks within which to situate what you are already doing in your classrooms in order to reveal what work needs to be done. This would mean asking yourself the following: In what ways am I already helping my students to learn language, to learn about language, to learn through language, and to use language to critique? Then build a literacy curriculum based on your responses.

How This Book Is Organized

It is important to reemphasize that my collaborators and I use books as only one of many tools for constructing critical literacies. However, books alone, even those books referred to as social issues texts (Harste et al., 2000)—such as texts that address topics of race, class, or gender—are useful as tools to do critical literacy work only in so far as they can be vehicles for discussing issues of power and control. Simply having these books available is not enough. What makes them social issues texts are the differences that the discourses or belief-laden ways of being and talking have on our discussion about those books and the experiences that influence those discussions, along with who is able to participate, in what ways, for what purposes, and to what ends. It is most advantageous to use such books in combination with other texts as a way of helping students to understand that texts are never neutral and that they are constructed for particular reasons and audiences.

In the following chapters you will be shown examples of how books have been paired with other texts, including everyday texts and media reports, to explore various topics and issues. What are central in each of the stories are the issues that the children raise about the world and the difference critical literacy discourse makes in each context. My collaborators and I also used children's literature to create space in our own contexts for making available to children more powerful discourses from which to frame discussion about books and everyday life events.

The focus of chapter 2 is on using everyday texts such as news reports and posters in combination with children's books to engage in social action. I share work I did with kindergarten students, while David Chiola-Nakai shares work done with his sixth-grade students.

In chapter 3 you will hear about Lee Heffernan and her third-grade students as they use a six-step strategy developed by Lee to take up particular social issues such as racism, using what Harste refers to as "social issues texts."

In chapter 4 you will learn about Susan Adamson's use of process drama and books written for children as a way to interrogate social inequities in an elementary school where she worked with seven third graders. You also will hear about work done by Janice Shear's fifth-grade students with regard to using a particular children's book in combination with process writing to construct meaning about inequities in their lives.

In chapter 5, Mike Muise sheds light on the work he did with fifth- and sixth-grade students when they used a picture book as a springboard for engaging critical literacies in the math curriculum.

Finally, discussed in chapter 6 is the notion of using language to critique as a common element underlying the work outlined in this book.

I hope that the version of classroom life that my collaborators and I present in the following chapters can complement or encourage the vision you have for engaging in powerful ways with texts in order to create spaces for a more equitably just and fair world for children.

Chapter 2

Pairing Everyday Texts With Texts Written for Children

Curtis:	*Who are those again?*
Patrick:	*Oh, Mounties.*
Julia:	*When I grow up I can be one!*
Roger:	*When I grow up I will be a horse.*
Emily:	*You can't be a horse; you're a person not an animal!*
Curtis:	*No, you can't! There are no girl Mounties in the poster.*

This conversation took place in my kindergarten classroom. The children were referring to a poster of the Royal Canadian Mounted Police (RCMP), which they were using to discuss who could or could not be an RCMP officer. Another student, Jessica, initiated the discussion when she noticed there were no females in the poster. The RCMP, also referred to as Mounties, is Canada's national police force that was founded more than 125 years ago to enforce the law during Canada's early settlement days. Today the RCMP acts as the municipal police force in about 200 Canadian cities and towns.

During the year that the above discussion took place, the parents of one of the children in my class were RCMP officers. As such, they were able to arrange for another officer to visit with the children. After the visit, the officer left a poster of the Mounties' musical ride team on horseback on a bulletin board in the classroom. The opening conversation took place as the children began to look closely at the poster while they worked on their various class projects.

Manning (1993) talks about three curricula that play out in the classroom: the mandated curriculum, which is provided by the school district head offices; the paper curriculum, which consists of the curriculum guides that are often part of prepackaged programs; and the real curriculum, which refers to the issues and topics raised by students in classrooms. The conversation at the opening of this chapter represents the real curriculum. Anything that students and/or teachers bring to the classroom has the potential to become the real curriculum. This curriculum and what children learn from it in terms of skills and content often intersect with the paper and mandated curriculum. It simply looks and sounds different. As the classroom teacher, I took it upon myself to keep track of ways in which this real curriculum complemented or connected with what was required by the school board. What makes the real curriculum

---

Box 2.1
Everyday Texts—What Are They?

Everyday texts are

- Texts that are spoken or written as part of everyday life.
- Texts that are so common that we don't carefully take notice of them.

We are less aware of the kinds of messages about our world that are conveyed by everyday texts. Because these are not natural representations of the world, they can be deconstructed and analyzed to uncover the view of the world they represent to make visible the lifestyles and identities that are constructed through what is presented and through how it is presented.

Resources to Learn More About Everyday Texts

Granville, S. (1993). *Language, advertising, and power*. Johannesburg, South Africa: Witwatersrand University Press.

Janks, H. (1993). *Language identity and power*. Johannesburg, South Africa: Witwatersrand University Press.

Newfield, D. (1993). *Words and pictures*. Johannesburg, South Africa: Witwatersrand University Press.

O'Brien, J. (1994). Show Mum you love her: Taking a new look at junk mail. *Reading*, *28*(1), 43–46.

Rule, P. (1993). *Language and the news*. Johannesburg, South Africa: Witwatersrand University Press.

Vasquez, V. (2000). Building community through social action. *School Talk*, *5*(4), 2–3.

Vasquez, V., & Egawa, K. (Eds.). (2002). Everyday texts, everyday literacies. *School Talk*, *8*(1), 1–8.

sound and look different are the different ways of talking that are brought to bear on the issues raised by children. These different ways of talking, or discourses, provide alternate frameworks through which children can speak about the world around them.

In this chapter, the focus is on the kind of work that can be accomplished when everyday texts (see Box 2.1 for information on everyday texts) are paired with books written for children and what happens when alternate discourses are used to engage in discussion about these texts.

Reflection Point 2.1

Take a survey of all the everyday texts that your students bring to school. After reading this chapter, look at your survey and jot down some ways to construct curricular opportunities using such texts.

You Can Be a Mountie When You Grow Up

Jessica:	There's no girls. There's no girls in it.
Roger:	There's men.
Nicholas:	'Cause there's horses.
Teacher:	Let's talk about that for a minute. A lot of you have been saying there are no girls in it. What does that tell you? What does this poster say about being a girl Mountie?
Andrea:	Well, ummm, one time my dad went up a mountain and there was only girls in it. There was no boys.
Teacher:	Oh, really. So there was another—so in that case there were only girls and no boys. Is that what you're saying?
Patrick:	Because there's boys and men and there's no girls because ummm, girls are not like boys are they?

Teacher:	So do you mean that you don't think they can do this job? That being a Mountie is a boy thing to do? Does anyone have anything they'd like to say about that?
Girls:	Yeah!
Jessica:	Well, my dad. He lets me ride on his back when he's pretending to be a horse to try and catch my brother Kyle. Well, since I know something like I go on my merry-go-round at Woodbine and at Square One [shopping malls], that it tells me that I could go on it too 'cause I know how to ride like girls 'cause both feet on one side and then you ride. But on real horses you gotta hold tight and do the same.
Kyle:	Ummm, I went on the merry-go-round at Square One and that tells me that ummm, ummm, that I like horses and I ride one horse but not with these men on it. I didn't wear the hat like that or the coats.
Andrea:	One time I went on a real horse. My daddy helped me. When I went on the horse I was just three years old and I—it was the sister. When she was four years old she fell in front of her horsy.
Jessica:	Well, girls, they can take boys' place even if they don't know how to hammer and all that 'cause my mom, dad he works with wood down in the basement to finish it and mom she helps and I'm a girl right? So I help too. Well, once dad I think was sick, but he didn't tell me the rest 'cause I don't think he was feeling well when he didn't tell me the rest. 'Cause a girl took his place, and he had to get off work 'cause he was starting to bleed or he was sick to get off work.
Teacher:	And a girl took his place?
Jessica:	Yeah.
Teacher:	What do you think about that?
Jessica:	I think that girls could ride horses too!

The Mountie poster, which began a class conversation about how girls/females are constructed by social text, represents one way in which males are privileged in society. If the previous conversation had not taken place, it is possible that this poster would have remained, implicitly stabilizing an inequitable distribution of power between males and females. The comments made by Andrea, "Well, ummm, one time my dad went up a mountain and there was only girls in it. There was no boys" and Patrick, "Because there's boys and men and there's no girls because ummm, girls are not like boys are they?" begin to tease at the students' perception of how boys and girls, and men and women, are positioned by everyday texts such as the poster. Andrea cites an example of an all-girls situation to counter the all-boys Mountie poster. Patrick makes a statement that girls are not like boys, implicitly reasoning that there are no girls in the poster because girls are not like boys. Patrick's statement could lead to the conclusion that girls are not capable of being Mounties because there is something they cannot do that boys are able to do.

As the conversation continued, making problematic the absence of women in the poster, traditional notions of femininity were challenged and traditional male and female roles destabilized. Jessica began to construct her model of possibility for girls and women as she drew from her personal experience of riding horses, "I know something like I go on my merry-go-round at Woodbine and at Square One, that it tells me that I could go on it too 'cause I know how to ride like girls 'cause both feet on one side and then you ride. But on real horses you gotta hold tight and do the same." This was her way of problematizing the absence of females in the Mountie poster, implicitly arguing that girls can ride horses and, therefore, should have been represented in the poster. Jessica made her stance explicit when she declared, "I think that girls could ride horses too!" meaning that females, therefore, also could be Mounties.

In response to this conversation, my students and I searched through our school library for information about the Mounties. One book that the children were most interested in due to the clear, bold illustrations was *The Royal Canadian Mounted Police* written and illustrated by Marc Tetro (1994). The cover of the book depicts a group of five Mounties—some short, others tall, all of them sporting mustaches, all of them male. Immediately, comments were made by both boys and girls in the class regarding this book cover being "just the same" as the poster—they both "mean the same" and "tell us the same." One of the girls asked, "Why?" meaning why do the book cover and poster both exclude women?

While reading the book, another illustration caught the group's attention. The illustration clearly depicted why the Mountie poster was designed as it was—depicting an all-male police force. The text read, "Among the recruits [RCMP recruits] there were teachers and farmers, students and lumberjacks." All the recruits were male. Some of the children were puzzled by what the text meant but made connections to the poster while looking closely at the illustration. One of the children decided that the person in front must be the farmer because "he is wearing overalls." Someone else decided that a person in the back row must be the student because "the bag he is carrying looks like a backpack." They couldn't decide on which character the lumberjack could be because "what does a lumberjack look like anyway?" They also could not figure out which character the teacher could be because none of them "look like Ms. Vasquez." It was interesting to see the children use their previous experiences—their available cultural capital and ways of being (discourses) that were familiar to them—to construct meaning from the illustrations.

Reflection Point 2.2

Together with your students, look through the books you have available in the classroom and list the various roles given to male and female characters. Discuss with your students ways of rewriting some of the stories to create alternate versions.

As I continued reading the book, I watched as Andrea and Jessica moved closer to me. "Wait, Wait, Wait.... It's the same again, it's all men and no girls." Women had no part in the history of the RCMP as represented by Tetro's book. I asked them to consider what could have been given to women and girls as responsibilities during the times when the Mounties were first introduced. We looked at some reference books of that time period to see if men were given all the jobs that people thought were "important." The children shared examples of women they know who are doctors or lawyers, citing that "Ms. Vasquez is a teacher and she's a girl so it's not exactly the same as before." They were learning that history is a social construction, that previous ways of being can be changed, and that as we live our lives we are in fact writing history.

Picking up on this comment, I shared that there are more jobs taken by women in recent years that have not been available to them in the past. I also shared that this change took a long time and that many women over the years worked hard at making sure that women today have different opportunities. I told them about Emily Stowe, who fought for the rights of women to be admitted to medical school in the 1800s, and Clara Martin, who fought for the rights of women to enter the legal profession. My students and I also talked about how historical constructions, as in the case of the Mounties originally being an all-male group, can easily be maintained and how that might happen. Further discussion took place regarding the need to continue to find ways to make sure that men and women are treated equitably and that women and girls are given the same kinds of opportunities that men are given. Jessica interjected with "and this poster and this book does not make things equal." This comment led to a conversation regarding the need to look critically at the way women and girls are represented in different texts like the poster. As a class we read other books that presented different ways of being (different positionings) for females. Some of the books included *Mama Is a Miner*, *The Paper Bag Princess*, and *Princess Smartypants*. We also read and discussed books in which females were marginalized such as *Counting on Frank* and *Piggybook*. All of these books gave us a perspective from which to read magazine fliers and other everyday texts, such as food packaging and toy packaging, and to watch television shows.

My students and I also talked about doing what we could to help change the way certain groups such as girls and women are positioned in society. In response to our conversations, Andrea—whose parents are both in the RCMP—spoke up saying that if they (Mounties) "keep sending this poster out then some people, like girls, won't know that they can be Mounties too."

Box 2.2
Books for Children That Can Be Used to Discuss Gender Issues

Browne, A. (1986). *Piggybook*. New York: Knopf.

Buehner, C. (1996). *Fanny's dream*. New York: Dial.

Clement, R. (1991). *Counting on Frank*. Milwaukee, WI: Gareth Stevens.

Cole, B. (1997). *Princess Smartypants*. New York: Putnam.

dePaola, T. (1979). *Oliver Button is a sissy*. San Diego: Harcourt Brace Jovanovich.

Hoffman, M. (1991). *Amazing Grace*. New York: Dial.

Lyon, G. (1994). *Mama is a miner*. New York: Scholastic.

Maury, I. (1976). *My mother the mail carrier/Mi mama la cartera*. New York: Feminist Press.

Miller, W. (1994). *Zora Hurston and the Chinaberry tree*. New York: Low Books.

Munsch, R. (1986). *The paper bag princess*. Toronto: Annick Press.

Schroeder, A. (2000). *Minty: A story of young Harriet Tubman*. New York: Puffin.

Zipes, J. (Ed.). (1989). *Don't bet on the prince: Contemporary feminist fairy tales in North America*. New York: Routledge Kegan & Paul.

Zolotow, C. (1972). *William's doll*. New York: Harper & Row.

As our conversation continued, it became clear that, historically, various texts have worked in favor of boys and men. Our conversation implicitly became a way of countering this historical effect and finding ways to have text work differently for girls and women (see Box 2.2 for information on books that can be used to discuss gender issues).

Constructing Alternate Realities

Of all the students in the class, Jessica seemed most eager to take action against the inequities discussed in the classroom. She decided that she needed to show the Mounties what the poster should look like today, "because today, women are Mounties also." In other words, they not only should be given the opportunity to become RCMP but, in fact, already are in position as RCMP officers; therefore, their presence should be recognized. She called her poster "My Poster of the Way the Mountie Poster Should Be" (see Figure 4). In Jessica's poster there are an equitable number of men and women represented. Once completed, she asked me to help her with a letter to the Mounties (see Figure 5). Jessica decided to

Figure 4
Jessica's Mountie Poster

Figure 5
Jessica's Letter

The letter reads,
Could you please change the
poster because there
are girls in the Mounties (police force).

send both the letter and the poster to the RCMP office in the city where she lived.

A few weeks after having posted her letter and poster, the father of one of the children in another class, who was a RCMP officer, approached me and asked if someone from my class had sent a letter to the RCMP. He then proceeded to share that no one had ever pointed out the inequity in the poster before. When I asked what action would be taken as a result of Jessica's letter, he replied by saying that if those in charge of media promotions do not do anything to resolve this issue that the women in his department certainly would. This Mountie story became a metaphor for the way in which my students and I read different texts in our classroom. This included everyday texts such as the Mountie poster and books written for children. No longer did the children read blindly, accepting how texts construct them; they began to realize how text could be reconstructed in more equitable ways not only for boys and girls, men and women, but for people or groups who have been marginalized, disadvantaged, or discriminated against.

Reflection Point 2.3

Look closer at one of the everyday texts you surveyed at the beginning of this chapter. Jot down some ways that you could support your students in redesigning that text to represent an alternate reality as Jessica did with her redesign of the Mountie poster.

In the next section of this chapter, you will meet David Chiola-Nakai and his class of 32 sixth-grade students in a Catholic school in the greater Toronto area of Ontario, Canada, and hear about ways that they used media text along with text written for children as one way to create space for critical literacy.

Pairing Media Texts With Texts Written for Children

Teacher:	What are the "uniforms" that kids wear in school?
Victor:	What do you mean?
Teacher:	Well, what kinds of clothes do "cool" kids wear? How do we know when someone is cool?
Tomislav:	Cool kids wear Nike.
Others:	Nike is the best. Yeah! Nike rules!

Like my kindergarten students and me, David Chiola-Nakai and his sixth-grade students also worked with everyday texts in combination with books written for children. The above conversation was part of a discussion following a read-aloud of *The Hockey Story* by R.J. Childerhose (1981). The story is about a hockey game between a team from an urban area and one from a rural area. David's students were immediately drawn to the obvious difference between the two teams' uniforms. The team from the city wore matching uniforms and was outfitted from helmet to skates. The team from the rural area wore a ragtag mix of whatever equipment and uniforms they could find. This contrast in the resources available to each team led David, together with his students, to discuss inequity and the different ways that people can position one another in classist ways, including judging someone based on the clothes he or she wears. As part of that conversation, they discussed what clothing is considered "cool" and wondered who determines what is "cool." The opening conversation took place as part of the discussion on this topic.

Bigelow et al. (1994) state "if we ask students to critique the world but then fail to encourage them to act, our classrooms can degenerate into factories for cynicism" (p. 4). In other words, critique void of action does not lead to change. The only thing it can lead to is the creation of cynics who talk about what is wrong with the world without contributing to changing that world. David recognized that he could capitalize on his students' interest in Nike to engage in critical literacy that could lead to some sort of social action. The following exchange took place even before he could begin to address the notion of taking action in the world to change inequitable ways of being.

Tomislav: But Nike is all over the world. How can we make a change?

Victor: We could stop buying their products.

Mike: I'll never stop buying Nike!

It became clear to David that engaging in critical literacy work could cause tension in the classroom. Some of his students were clearly expressing anticorporate agenda sentiments, while others treasured the cultural capital that came with being a Nike wearer.

Finding comfort in the notion that tension is a great propeller of learning, David forged on regardless of the tensions he began to face regarding how to enact a critical curriculum.

Reflection Point 2.4

Tape record some of the discussions that you have with your students. While playing back the recording, take note of tensions that are evident in the children's comments and questions. Reflect on how you might use these tensions as one way of motivating learning in your classroom.

A Nike Story: Using Tensions to Propel Learning

> A social system can only be held in place by the meanings the people make of it. Culture is deeply inscribed in the differential distribution of power within a society, for power relations can only be stabilized or destabilized by the meanings that people make of them. Culture is a struggle for meanings as society is a struggle for power. (Fiske, 1989, p. 20)

According to Fiske (1989), a social system or a society's accepted ways of being are maintained through use. The important question is, Who decides on what systems to maintain and use and for what purposes? Who gets to do what, however, is rooted in who has or does not have power to act in particular ways. Fiske refers to this as a differential distribution of power.

David wondered how Fiske's notion of the differential distribution of power intersected with the issue of classism and inequity his students had raised. He realized that not acting on these issues in some way or at least making visible to his students possible ways of taking action would mean that he and his students would be contributing to maintaining inequitable ways of being.

While attempting to figure out how to deal with his students' struggle for meaning, David mentioned their conversation regarding Nike to one of his colleagues, who proceeded to tell him about a television report on Nike's mistreatment of factory workers in developing countries. In response, David asked if she could talk to his class and share what she had seen. At that time, he had not realized the generativeness of connecting everyday text such as the television segment with the original conversations regarding equity in *The Hockey Story.*

David: *I began to sense my students' growing awareness of the overwhelming presence Nike had in their lives. They began to take much more notice of the plethora of Nike gear worn in the school. I heard disbelief in their voices as they began to discuss issues of fair wages and child labor and the role that we play as consumers in maintaining children as laborers when we consume Nike products. Posters appeared on the classroom walls depicting anti-Nike sentiments. Similar to the way it has come to dominate the sports world, the Nike sports empire suddenly became the focus of a classroom study.*

I could feel the sense of being overwhelmed by the idea of taking on such a huge conglomerate. Imagine a group of 11- to 12-year-old students taking on the giant of the sports world. But as Harste has said, history is replete with examples of "tripping the giant" (1997, p. 2).

What started as a conversation around a children's book turned into a discussion around issues of power and consumerism when the issues raised in the book were paired with the inequities made visible in a television segment.

Creating Spaces for Students to Think Differently

David: *I started to see how the classroom could offer space for analyzing the daily texts that students bring to school. I realized that spaces for conversation on social issues could come from an assortment of texts, not just books. I think I was beginning to further my understanding of interrogating texts and how to make them problematic. I could also see how the classroom was becoming a safe zone for my students to critically analyze the world around them. Not everyone took the same position. Many remained loyal to Nike and refused to stop wearing the brand name's clothing or shoes. Others engaged in a personal boycott, stripping their bodies of any sort of Nike wear to symbolize their protest against the corporation's treatment of their workers.*

David found himself caught in the whirlwind of events happening in and out of the classroom. His role became blurred as he found himself in the position of both a resource and a learner. He searched the papers and magazines to provide articles and materials to support his students' inquiries and found new ways of using existing learning tools and strategies (see Box 2.3 for resources on media literacy).

David: *I began to see how we could use surveys and graphing, investigating maps and charts, money, letter writing, learning logs, posters, questionnaires, response logs, and presentations in our investigations. For example, two students designed a survey to find out the approximate number of hats, shoes, and shirts that were owned by students in our school and how many of these were Nike products. They took the information and drew graphs and reported what they had discovered to the rest of the class to show the predominance of Nike consumers. They then went on to do a presentation to our reading buddies, first-grade students with whom we read picture books once a week, about Nike's mistreatment of workers. I found this helped my students to articulate their concerns better while at the same time disseminating information they thought was important.*

Many students designed posters depicting anti-Nike sentiment. These were alternate versions of existing Nike ads. Two other students wrote a joint letter to Phillip Knight, CEO of Nike, asking him to tell Nike's side of the story on the use of child laborers and the use of sweatshops.

Reflection Point 2.5

Observe your students as they engage in small-group and class discussions.

1. What real-world issues are they raising? Make a list of these issues.

2. What kinds of texts might you use to inform class conversations about these issues? Jot down some thoughts regarding how you could negotiate these issues as curriculum.

Box 2.3
Resources on Media Literacy

Alverman, D.E., Moon, J.S., Hagood, M.C. (1999). *Popular culture in the classroom: Teaching and researching critical media literacy.* Newark, DE: International Reading Association; Chicago: National Reading Conference.

Buckingham, D. (1993). *Children talking television: The making of television literacy.* London: Routledge Falmer Press.

Buckingham, D., & Sefton-Green, J. (1995). *Cultural studies goes to school: Reading and teaching popular media.* London: Taylor & Francis.

Kavanagh, K. (1997). *Texts on television: School literacies through viewing in the first years of school.* Adelaide, South Australia: Department of Education and Children's Services.

Klein, N. (2000). *No logo: Taking aim at the brand name bullies.* Toronto: Vintage Canada Press.

McLaren, P., Hammer, R., Sholle, D., & Smith Reilly, S. (1995). *Rethinking media literacy: A critical pedagogy of representation.* New York: Peter Lang.

Comber (2001) notes,

> children are accustomed to thinking analytically about power and plea-sure.... The task for teachers is to help children to develop a meta-aware-ness and a meta-language for what they already know how to do and to assist them in applying these resources to the texts and situations of school life. The varying practices that different children bring with them can become part of a collective capacity to solve problems and approach possibilities. (p. 2)

Developing a collective capacity to solve problems and approach pos-sibilities is one of the goals that David had hoped could be accomplished through their class inquiry. The point of the inquiry was not to make peo-ple change their minds but to provide students with new ways of talking and thinking about "the everyday worlds of community, media, and lit-erature" (Comber, 2001, p. 2) to make informed critical decisions.

Reading text sets (see Box 2.4 for information on text sets) on a par-ticular topic can help students to understand that texts are never neutral, and that they are constructed by particular people with particular goals and motivations (Comber, 2001). In the case of the Nike inquiry for in-stance, David's students learned to read between the lines of Nike ads as well as media reports on Nike's corporate practices, which all started from the inequities that his students noticed in a story about a hockey game.

Box 2.4
Aspects of Text Sets

A text set is a group of books and other print and media materials such as magazine articles and video clips designed to support the study of a particular theme, genre, or issue. A set usually consists of at least four or five texts and should be carefully constructed to provide different perspectives. Sometimes these perspectives are complementary and other times they may be conflicting but nevertheless offer a way of viewing the same area under study.

Resources to Find Out More About Text Sets

Harste, J., Leland, C., Lewison, M., Ociepka, A., & Vasquez, V. (2000). Supporting critical conversations in classrooms. In K.M. Pierce (Ed.), *Adventuring with books* (pp. 507–512). Urbana, IL: National Council of Teachers of English.

Leland, C., Harste, J., Ociepka, A., Lewison, M., & Vasquez, V. (1999). Exploring critical literacy: You can hear a pin drop. *Language Arts, 77*(1), 70–77.

Short, K., Harste, J., & Burke, C. (1996). *Creating classrooms for authors and inquirers.* Portsmouth, NH: Heinemann.

Reflection Point 2.6 _____

In the latter part of this chapter, you read about David and the work that he and his students did to take up issues of classism and inequity. What they accomplished was a beginning. Reflect on some other strategies that David could have used to push his students' thinking further. For example, what other kinds of work could he have done to analyze advertisement fliers or television commercials?

In this chapter, David and I demonstrated how we paired children's books with everyday texts to develop social action projects with our students. Our hope was for our experiences to make visible the potential for learners to live critically literate lives regardless of age. My students were only 4 years old when they took on the Mountie poster as text. David's students were 11 and 12 years old. Both groups of learners, however, worked equally as hard at attempting to engage critical literacies in their own settings in an attempt to change inequitable ways of being. As a result of these experiences, as classroom teachers, David and I learned what it means for students to take social action as a result of using a critical literacy perspective in the classroom. It also became clear to us that this kind of work is not about telling people what to think or how to think but giving them opportunities to think about and discuss important social issues that matter in their lives from different perspectives. In the next chapter, you will meet Lee Heffernan and her students and learn about a particular strategy she used to make curriculum critical.

Chapter 3

Focusing on Social Issues:
Bringing the Outside World
Into the Classroom

Ben:	*Do you notice that most main characters are white and stuff?*
Louis:	*In lots of movies, most of the main characters are white.*
Kristen:	*When you look in a book...no black people.*
John:	*Yeah.*
Kristen:	*When you look in a book, it's like, they're white, they're white, there and there and there...and like off in the distance, you find one African American girl.*

The school year was nearly over. One late May morning, the children in Lee Heffernan's third-grade public school classroom in a U.S. midwestern town gathered at the rug to discuss *White Wash*, a picture book by Ntozake Shange. The book was one of several social issues books Lee shared with her students. She defines social issues books as those books that deal specifically with topics such as racism or gender equity (see Appendix B). The previous exchange is part of one of many conversations that took place as Lee and her students discussed their comments, questions, and connections about such books. She notes that discussions she has had with her students about these books were not like those she has had with them in the past, claiming her students brought up issues that were difficult to understand and sometimes uncomfortable to discuss.

The book *White Wash* is about a young African American girl, Helene-Angel, who is attacked by the Hawks—a white gang—who spray paint her face white while she walks home from school with her older brother Mauricio. Traumatized by the incident, Helene-Angel finds sanctuary in her bedroom where she feels safe. Her grandmother understands how Helene-Angel feels having experienced similar treatment in the South when she was younger, so she encourages her granddaughter to come out of her room and be strong. When she does, Helene-Angel finds her classmates waiting to walk her to school in a show of support.

As Lee read the book, her students eagerly anticipated an opportunity for response. From their previous experience studying picture books with Lee, they knew that the book would be the focus of their reading and writing minilesson work for several days. Lee used minilessons as a way of teaching specific concepts about a topic, unpacking or analyzing texts such as books, or teaching specific skills.

When she first began reading books that focused on social issues, Lee was surprised by the complex conversations that resulted. Although she was initially hesitant to share such books, the children responded with such enthusiasm that she came to see books as important tools for bringing a critical perspective to the reading and writing workshop.

Lee: *I began by spending several days talking about the books and came to see that lingering with a book over several days had some benefits. First, we were able to talk about a wide range of issues, rather than focusing on one or two main ideas or themes. Second, kids who tended to be quieter found their voice after several days and shared insights that we would have missed. Third, I was able to give myself more time to consider and develop issues from the book that seemed especially significant to all of us.*

Reflection Point 3.1

Reflect on the various kinds of books you share with your students. From those books, what kinds of social issues or topics do the children have opportunities to discuss?

Lingering With a Book:
Six Sessions With a Social Issues Text

Like Lisa Stanzi's students in the Kids InSight book *Looking Through the Faraway End: Creating a Literature-Based Reading Curriculum With Second Graders* (Galda, Rayburn, & Stanzi, 2000), Lee's students did not come to school knowing how to talk to one another about books. One of the ways she taught them this skill was by giving them sustained time to linger with a book. She developed a series of engagements for sharing and studying picture books that she called "six sessions for working with a

---

Box 3.1
Lee's Six Sessions for Working With a Picture Book

Session 1: Read Aloud
Read the book out loud and give students ample time to make connections, comment, and ask questions.

Session 2: Picture Walk
Small groups meet to discuss the book and fill out a response sheet that includes the following prompts:
- What is important to remember about this book?
- What surprised you about this book?
- What questions do you have?
- Name a possible writing topic from your own life that relates to the book.

The teacher then compiles all the students' questions on one sheet.

Session 3: Small-Group Conversations
Different groupings of students meet to discuss the question list generated from the response sheets. Then groups monitor their responses to the questions by putting a check next to questions that did not generate much conversation and a star next to questions that were discussed at length.

Session 4: Whole-Group Meeting
The class meets as a whole group to discuss the starred questions.

Session 5: Choose an Illustration
The group discusses the illustration from the book that best represents the conversations about it. Once an illustration is selected, it is posted on the learning wall (Vasquez, 1999) along with a caption.

Session 6: Notebook Writing
Each student writes a couple of pages in his or her notebook about the writing topics noted on the response sheet during session 2. These entries are later revisited to determine potential topics to develop further.

picture book" (see Box 3.1). She referred to these sessions as minilessons, which she used during readers' or writers' workshop. While discussing the implementation of the six-sessions strategy, Lee commented, "Sometimes I don't go through all six sessions with every book we read together. Sometimes I change the order of the activities or alter them in some way, depending on topics that come up during our conversations."

Lee noted that the number of days it took to go through the various sessions really depended on the book under study. Here, Lee details how she used the six-sessions strategy while working with the book *White Wash*.

Session 1: Reading Aloud

Lee: *I chose* White Wash *to read out loud in response to earlier conversations about how much, or how little, power children have in society. The book seemed to extend the idea of kids taking action with its message of kids working togeth- er as a group to protect a classmate. Previously, I had shared texts that focused on young people participating in some form of social action.* (See Appendix C for an annotated list of books in which characters take social action.)

As I began reading, the class became focused and quiet. When I got to the scene in the book that described the attack, Quinn interrupted, "You tell us not to write violent stories, so how come you're reading us this book with violence in it?"

Quinn was referring to a previous conversation from when Lee and the third graders read a series of books on human rights. She had shared two picture books about slavery, along with several other titles. Moved by the slavery texts, half the children chose to write slave narratives as they created their own picture book on human rights. Quinn and some other boys had focused on the violence of slavery. Lee suggested to them that their narratives ought to include elements of hope and not to focus solely on violence. Lee responded to Quinn's comment by stating, "This book has more than violence to it. You'll see what I mean at the end."

Session 2: Picture Walk

Lee: *While revisiting the book for a second time, I began with a "picture walk" through the text. (During a picture walk students talk about the storyline of a book by discussing the illustrations.) I then had the children work with a part- ner to fill out a response prompt sheet (see Figure 6). I change the response sheet as needed, but in general it contains the same four to six "prompts."*

Figure 6
Response Prompt Sheet

Why do you think people should or should not read *White Wash*?	What questions do you have about this story?
What surprised you about this book?	Write one or two writing topics from your own life that connect with this story.
Write one or two statements from someone whose perspective is represented in this book.	Write one or two statements from someone whose perspective is not represented in the book.

I added a new prompt, "Why do you think people should or should not read White Wash*?" to the response sheet for* White Wash *after I thought about Quinn's comments regarding the violence in the book. Prompts are statements or questions that help the children begin to unpack the book. The kids worked with partners to answer the prompts.*

Examples of student responses are included in Figure 7. Lee collated the responses on a single sheet of paper for use in subsequent discussions.

Figure 7
Some Responses to the *White Wash* Prompt Sheet

Why do you think people should or should not read *White Wash*?	What questions do you have about this story?
• It shows that there are some people that do some really bad things. • You should read it because it teaches you to stick up for others. It has kid power in it!	• If the girl were white, would the Hawks be mean to her? • Why did she stay in her room for so long?
What surprised you about this book?	Write one or two writing topics from your own life that connect with this story.
• That the bad people would paint her face white. • I was surprised that they let go of the brother first. • Everything!	• My brother is always mean to me and beats me up. • When I got stitches on my chin, I looked like I had a beard. I had to go to school like that. • Being mad
Write one or two statements from someone whose perspective is represented in this book.	Write one or two statements from someone whose perspective is not represented in the book.
• (Helene-Angel) I don't want to go outside! They'll bully me again! • (Helene-Angel) I'm hungry, but I can't eat. I hope I can stand up to them next time. • (Brother) I cannot believe I let those boys push my sister around.	• (Brother) Run! Leave her alone! • (Gang member) Man, those stupid kids think they can protect her. Ha! • (Gang member) That shows them! It proves white people are better than black people.

Session 3: Small-Group Conversations

Lee: *While I usually read over the list with the kids and then send them off for small-group conversations, I decided to begin by following up on Quinn's comments about violence in* White Wash. *We read the list of reasons for either reading the book or for censoring the book. Some of the reasons noted by the children for reading* White Wash *were*

- *It shows that there are some people that do some really bad things.*
- *It's a good book.*
- *It teaches you to stick up for others. It has kid power in it!*

As the children reviewed the list, Lee asked them to put a check mark beside any statements that connect in some way to any stories they had written previously. Will immediately shared that both books he wrote in class were about sticking up for other people. Robbie noted his story was about kid power in which two teenagers escape from being slaves.

Next, Lee and her students used writing to think about inequitable ways of being in the world. At every opportunity, she tried to point out the power in writing about important themes and issues from their lives as one way of uncovering how they may have contributed to maintaining inequitable ways of being and as a way to come up with possibilities for changing inequities in the world.

After a brief discussion about how readers can benefit from reading *White Wash*, Lee asked her students if they thought the book should be censored and why.

Robbie:	I think the book is violent, but not too violent.
Will:	Well it's not...I mean it's not like gory and all bloody. They didn't describe it like, "oh look at his bloody arm."
Teacher:	I see. There's a difference?
Will:	It does have some violence, but not as much as some other things.
Teacher:	What's something that has a lot of violence, gory violence?
John:	*Scream 2.*

Mark:	*Halloween.*
Tasha:	*Men in Black* has some violence.
Teacher:	So you think the violence in *White Wash* is different than the violence in these movies?

In this exchange, the children make a distinction between exploring violence in order to explore its consequences and exploring violence for the sake of grossing people out with blood and gore. This discussion about violence in books and movies signified to Lee that her students understood the difference between gratuitous violence and the violence used by authors to depict reality.

Lee: *In retrospect, I wish I had talked more about this issue of violence, focusing more deeply on differences between violence in the newspaper and violence in movies. Also, I could have discussed in greater detail the impact of reading about violence and using violence in our writing. I've come to accept these moments of 20/20 hindsight as part of a critical literacy curriculum. While I work to become more skillful at guiding critical conversations, I also have a greater awareness that conversations are not scripted entities. They have a life and spirit of their own.*

After some time, the children were asked to continue their discussion in small groups. Lee had them discuss the list of questions they had about the story from the response sheet. She collated the questions on a sheet of paper and handed out copies to each group. Throughout the year, her students had become very familiar with this process, evaluating questions in terms of how much conversation each generates. The children knew to put a check mark next to questions that did not generate much conversation and a star next to questions that were discussed at length. Lee noticed that this strategy helped her students develop substantive comments for literature circle discussions. During literature circles, small groups of children discuss various topics or issues connected to a particular book they are reading. For example, as Lee's students moved through the list of questions for *White Wash*, one group of three girls and one boy covered a wide range of topics including racism, the issue of the main character's "embarrassment" over what has happened to her, the motivation of the gang members, and children protecting one another.

Session 4: Whole-Group Meeting

During session 4, Lee brought the class together to go over the response list one more time in order to deal with the issue of embarrassment and shame, which was an issue raised during session 3.

Brad:	She was embarrassed because they put paint all over her face and she didn't want to go to school. She might have thought that all the kids...
Brenda:	She was afraid.
Kevin:	Like when she walked into school, they'd probably be all laughing.
Teacher:	People might laugh about it?
Kevin:	Yeah.
Lisa:	Well, I think that she might not want to go out because they could have done something a lot worse. They still could do something worse to her.
Will:	Maybe she was just embarrassed because she didn't want to face them [her friends].
John:	Maybe because she let someone paint her face white, instead of running away.
Kristen:	Like she might be afraid that her friends would be like, you let a white person attack you like that?
Teacher:	Do you think her friends would do that?
Kristen:	No, but she might think that.
Lisa:	She did say, "I'm an embarrassment to the whole race."
Brad:	And people might say, "You let people paint your face white? And you're trying to be white?" Because I mean, if they didn't know what happened?
Hank:	Maybe if they didn't know how it had happened.
Teacher:	Well, her friends did support her.
Quinn:	At the end.

According to Lee, the issue of shame came up many times in their discussions.

Lee: *It's a difficult issue for me. I tried to focus on the importance of awareness while acknowledging that these topics were emotional and often uncomfortable. There were no easy answers to these questions. While I guided the conversation, I considered myself a participant as we explored issues that troubled all of us. It was clear to me that the kids were ready to talk about the gritty issues in* White Wash. *They were not glossing over the issues in the text, but confronting them head on. They were not simply summarizing or merely asking why. They brought in connections from their own lives, the media, other books, and from previous conversations we've had.*

Reflection Point 3.2

In your journal, list some books or other texts that you know raise social issues. Reflect on your existing curriculum and identify some spaces in which you could try using Lee's six-session strategy.

Session 5: Choose an Illustration

During session 5, Lee asked her students to gather together to choose an illustration from the book to post on the learning wall (Vasquez, 1999). The learning wall is a large, floor-to-ceiling bulletin board in the classroom that holds important artifacts from the school year—photographs, souvenirs from field trips, newspaper headlines, and more (refer to Box 3.2 for resources on the learning wall). Each time Lee read a social issue picture book, she and her students chose an illustration from the book to remind them of their conversations. A caption was created to go along with each of the illustrations. Both were then posted on the learning wall.

Lee: *The students were familiar with this activity. I told them to think about which picture was most important as I picture walk through the pages of the book. They talked as they decided which illustration to post and defended their choices along the way. With some books, there was clear consensus among*

Box 3.2
Resources for Constructing a Learning Wall

Harste, J., Leland, C., Lewison, M., Ociepka, A., Vasquez, V. (2000). Supporting critical conversations in classrooms. In K. Mitchell Pierce (Ed.), *Adventuring with books*. Urbana, IL: National Council of Teachers of English.

Harste, J., & Vasquez, V. (1998). The work we do: Journal as audit trail. *Language Arts*, 75(4), 266–276.

Vasquez, V. (1999). *Negotiating critical literacies with young children*. Unpublished doctoral dissertation, Indiana University, Bloomington.

Vasquez, V. (2001). Creating a critical literacy curriculum with young children. *Phi Delta Kappa International Research Bulletin*. Bloomington, IN: Phi Delta Kappa.

Vasquez, V. (2001). Negotiating critical literacies in elementary classrooms. In B. Comber & A. Simpson (Eds.), *Critical literacy at elementary sites*. Mahwah, NJ: Erlbaum.

Vasquez, V. (2003). *Negotiating critical literacies with young children*. Mahwah, NJ: Erlbaum.

---

the kids. With others, kids chose a variety of illustrations. If no clear choice emerged, I picked a picture that connected with or highlighted our conversations. The conversations about which picture to choose reimmersed us in the text.

For White Wash *we selected the picture at the end of the book, in which all Helene-Angel's friends come to her house to escort her to school. Together we composed a caption for the picture. One student typed the caption in a large, colorful font and printed it. Another student mounted the picture and caption on construction paper. The page was laminated and stapled to the learning wall (Vasquez, 1999), which by this time of year was filled with striking illustrations from picture books as well as our own classroom artifacts. To me, it looked like a museum gallery or a giant collage. It helped visitors to our classroom know more about our class curriculum and helped us to reflect on our year together.*

Session 6: Notebook Writing

At writers' workshop later in the week, Lee returned the prompt sheets to her students. She then asked them to expand, in their writer's notebook, on the writing topics they identified in session 2. Lee's experience was that children frequently wanted to change their writing topic by this time because newer ideas had come up for them since the first few sessions.

The children were asked to write at least one page on their topic. When most of them appeared to be done, Lee asked the class to meet on the rug in a circle. Children who were not finished brought their notebooks with them to the rug and continued writing as they listened. The children then took turns sharing their writing. Those who were not ready for sharing had the option of passing, but everyone had to at least share his or her topic with the group. The topics often varied. Some were personal and fun while others were more sociological and serious.

Brad wrote about people making fun of his last name. Will wrote about face painting at the school carnival. Alice, an Asian American student, wrote about being called "Brownie" and "Blacky" by kids at school. Hank wrote about having to take care of his little brother. Meg wrote about her brother having an accident with a can of spray paint in their garage. Brenda wrote about her Sudanese neighbors, "I definitely would not paint their face white!" Kevin wrote about the time he was embarrassed to come to school with stitches in his chin. Blaire wrote about a shooting in the New York subway she had heard about on the news, "Why did someone shoot that person?"

Upon reflecting on session 6, Lee wrote in her journal,

> Our study of *White Wash* came at the end of the school year. Throughout the year, we had used the six-sessions chart with nearly 20 texts. Most of these were picture books, but we also used the chart to study chapter books and a video about social action. I used the six-sessions chart as a tool for allowing more voices to be heard in classroom conversations and for digging deeper into the real-world issues explored in these texts.

Reflection Point 3.3

Audiotape a discussion that you have with your students as you engage with a book.

- What kinds of questions are raised during these discussions?
- What do you do with the questions raised?
- How might Lee's strategy for sustaining conversation change the nature of your conversations?

In this chapter, Lee made visible the intertextuality of books as she showed how her students drew from their own experiences and their past experiences with texts to engage in powerful talk. As new issues emerged (violence in writing and media and the trauma of being victimized), the third graders extended their understanding of past topics (racism, shame, and social action). Using social issues texts in combination with other texts was a way to bring real-world issues into the classroom.

In the next chapter, we continue with Lee's notion of powerful talk in another third-grade classroom, as well as a fifth-grade classroom where Susan Adamson and Janice Shear share their use of children's books to unpack social issues in their school communities.

Chapter 4

Using Children's Literature to Unpack Social Issues in the School Community

Lauren:	*They're just watching!*
Teacher:	*Why are they just watching?*
Chase:	*Because they don't care what happens to black people.*
Teacher:	*What do you think? If you saw this out in the street, what would you want to do?*
Ethan:	*I'd kick their butt.*
Melissa:	*I'd call the police.*
Tommy:	*I'd beat them up and run.*
Teacher:	*You have to think of your own safety too, right?*
Melissa:	*They might have guns.*
Ethan:	*But what if they do have guns, you never know.*
Chase:	*Trip them and knock them out. Then say, "Who got the gun now?"*
Teacher:	*I'm asking you what you are able to do. You might want to go over there and beat them up, but you can't do that because you will probably get hurt.*
Lauren:	*But when someone's fighting like that you should go over there and help them.*
Teacher:	*How can you help? What can you do?*
Sean:	*Call the police!*
Tommy:	*You can talk them out of it.*
Emily:	*Okay, pretend I have a gun and I'm about to shoot you. What are you going to do? Talk me out of it. Talk me*

48

out of it. (She points her finger at him like it's a gun.)
I'm crazy. I'm drunk. Talk me out of it. I'm the one with
the gun. Talk me out of it.

While reflecting on this critical moment during a discussion with a group of third graders about the book *White Wash,* Susan Adamson noted,

> The children struggled with their sense of individual power and significance in relationship to their world. Their outrage was potent, a palpable strength of their knowing, but they were rendered impotent as no reasonable course of action occurred to them. Undaunted they continued to explore a repertoire of actions using their own personal text to guide them.

In what ways can children's books be used to create space for children to work through struggles regarding issues of power in their local settings? What kinds of strategies might classroom teachers put in place to help them make sense of that world? How might children use the texts of their everyday lives to read children's books? These are a few of the questions asked by Susan while she worked with a group of seven third-grade children in an urban public school in a midwestern U.S. town. Susan's reflection deals with her students' responses to the book and the difficulty they experienced when making sense of the racism presented in the text. In comparison to Lee Heffernan's work in the previous chapter, Susan makes use of process drama as she and her students use the book to engage in social action at their school site and to specifically address racism and violence.

In this chapter, you will meet Susan and her group of third graders as they focused on making sense of the world through interrogating and analyzing picture books in light of their own experiences. You will also meet Janice Shear and her fifth graders. The struggles with issues of power and control experienced by Susan, Janice, and their students will be addressed here. (See Appendix D for an annotated list of books for creating space to talk about issues of racism, power, and control.)

Acting Out: Using Process Drama to Read Critically

In her reflection, Susan commented on how the children undauntedly continued to explore their repertoire of possible actions. The children's repertoire of actions included using process drama as a way of constructing meaning and unpacking text. In this case, they unpack *White Wash* as did Lee Heffernan's students in the previous chapter. We deliberately chose not to focus on methods for engaging in process drama as this is not our intent with this chapter. Rather, we wanted to demonstrate one way in which students can draw from their past experiences—in this case what they already knew about "acting out" scenarios—to make sense of new experiences.

What is most interesting about Susan's work, as described in this chapter, is her venture into process drama as a tool to help her students use the book *White Wash* to address issues of violence and racism.

The opening discussion took place after Susan read *White Wash* to her group. Susan noted how the children overtly struggled with their sense of individual power and significance during the conversation. The conversation continued:

Ethan:	Scream bloody murder.
Melissa:	Say "fire," "fire!" That's what my Mom says to do.
Chase:	That's what my Mom says too. Even if they have a gun and tells you not to scream. You scream.
Emily:	What if they have a knife?
Teacher:	That's a really big dilemma because you have to decide whether or not to scream, and if you do they might harm you.

The children felt an urge to act out this scenario. They had already started to do this when Emily pretended to have a gun asking Tommy to "Talk me out of it." At first their dramatizations seemed futile as they ultimately dissolved into laughter.

Susan: *At this point Emily had assigned parts to the other students. While she played the part of "herself," she assigned two of the other boys to be her younger brothers and asked Tommy to be the "guy with the knife." Rather than situate them on the street as the children were in the story, her scenario had them in her house in one of the upstairs bedrooms. On her cue, the "brothers" began to cower in the corner while she tried to confront Tommy. As he slinked over, though, with his arm extended as if holding a knife, they all dissolved into laughter, falling on the floor or collapsing in a chair. But they quickly regrouped, clamoring to try new parts; "let me try, let me try" they shouted, as if they were more up to the task than the others were. At each attempt (two or three more), laughter prevailed.*

Reflection Point 4.1

Do you use process drama in your classroom as a way of responding to text? What aspects of drama do you think could be beneficial in your setting? In what ways could they be beneficial? How might you use drama to engage in critical literacy?

In spite of the laughter, the potential of using process drama to make explicit the children's tensions and anxieties was clear. While reflecting on this experience after the fact, Susan realized that the laughter reflected the children's anxiety with playing roles that had not been part of their schema. Previously they had used drama to act out scenes from books, but not as a way to problem solve while constructing new meaning. She noted that adding to the children's discomfort was their own sense of powerlessness in being unable to figure what to do when faced with such danger. Process drama provided an opportunity to represent the issues they struggled with using an alternate sign system that helped them act out the complexity of the issue at hand.

In response, Susan decided to propose an alternative. She wanted her students to be able to think more explicitly about their own feelings in relation to the inequalities of which they have direct experience (Epstein, 1993). They examined more closely the micropolitics of the playground in their school where they found similar dilemmas. Students relied on teachers to mediate conflicts but often found them to be unfair, ineffective, or unresponsive. This led to a study of behavior on the playground in which Susan and her seven students discussed their observations of negative interactions during recess. They were disturbed by what they saw. Acting on their belief that playground supervision needed to be revisited, they initiated a letter-writing campaign informing the principal of the crisis on the playground.

Luke and Freebody (1997) write that students bring to the classroom available cultural, community, and social resources, and texts and discourses. Said differently, all students come to school with cultural and social experiences and particular ways of saying and doing things. These various experiences, or cultural and linguistic resources, connect in multiple ways. What this means is learning environments need to be responsive to the cultural discourses that students have access to and are active in, by looking closely at the things that are important to them or that they feel have importance in their lives.

Susan: *The books we read and the conversations we had about those books made the cultural texts of the children I worked with easy to access. The books generated rich discussion of issues such as power, ageism, race, and gender. The students were comfortable expressing their ideas verbally; they appeared to speak openly and honestly. As such, our critical conversations offered several possible insights into how they were negotiating issues of social justice.*

According to Susan, in the third-grade classroom there was no shortage of opportunities to engage in important conversations about social justice and equity issues that stemmed from her students' lived experiences (refer to Box 4.1 for criteria in choosing books that create space for discussions regarding such issues). It was simply a matter of determining which conversation to pursue. Susan notes that as teachers we must keep in mind Epstein's (1993) notion of children as active in the construction of their own realities and subjectivities and, therefore, potentially active in the deconstruction of dominant ideologies. Dominant ideologies refer to prevalent societal beliefs. These ideologies are socially constructed; that is, they are created through social interactions between and among people. As such, they can be deconstructed and reconstructed.

Susan: *There are clearly many complicating factors in the construction of meaningful ideologies, but giving credence to one's own experience would seem*

> ## Box 4.1
> ## Criteria for Choosing Books That Create Space for Discussions Regarding Issues of Social Justice and Equity (Harste et al., 2000)
>
> They don't make difference invisible, but rather explore what differences make a difference.
>
> They explore dominant systems of meaning that operate in our society to position people in particular ways.
>
> They create space for taking action on important social issues.
>
> They help us to unpack our understanding of history by giving us an opportunity to hear from those who have been traditionally silenced or marginalized.
>
> They help us to question why certain groups are positioned as "other."

crucial to empowerment and lead to the deconstruction of dominant ideologies. This is at least part of what I understand critical literacy intends to do.

The cultural climate of this school has yet to challenge these students to analyze their beliefs in a way that lets them create their own well-considered belief systems. They were articulate and empathetic regarding issues of social justice and equity, and they saw a flawed system in which their counterpart, the adult, did not always support them. So while they seemed predisposed to act, they were not able to do so because there was no "space" for social action and, therefore, no space for the creation of alternative ideologies. But given the opportunity, these children would surely find their voices. And given their voices, we surely must listen.

Reflection Point 4.2

With your students, brainstorm a list of "things that matter," that is, issues or topics that are important to the group. Use the list to reflect on the topics or issues from which you create curriculum. Are the "things that matter" to your students reflected in your paper curriculum? In what ways might you be able to keep your students' interests "in sight" by negotiating the things that matter to them as curriculum?

Writing Out: Using Writing to Read Critically

After reading Toni and Slade Morrison's *The Big Box* (1999), Janice Shear's self-contained fifth-grade gifted students in Mississauga, Ontario, Canada, expressed sentiments similar to Susan's students with regard to social systems that they felt take freedom away from children.

The book has a haunting message about children who fall outside socially accepted norms. In poetic form, the authors tell the stories of Patty, Mickey, and Lisa Sue who "live in a big brown box" with "doors that open only one way." The adults responsible for these children felt that their behavior required they be locked away because they are unable to handle their freedom. While reflecting on her students' initial reaction to the book, Janice wrote,

> As I closed the book there was an audible sigh from the class. The kids, blink-
> ing at each other as if newly awakened from a dream, started some quiet talk,
> which quickly picked up momentum. The spell had been broken, reality re-
> entered, ideas surfaced. They talked among themselves and repeatedly
> chanted a line from the book, "they just can't handle their freedom."
>
> They asked me to read the book again. This time they anticipated
> my reading of the line, chanting repeatedly as I read on.

After first reading *The Big Box* aloud to her class, Janice described her students' being delighted with the line "they just can't handle their free-dom" as somewhat problematic. She felt that they did not take the book seriously. Nevertheless, Janice persisted in discussing the book further, and when they did, the tone of the children's conversation changed.

Janice: *After the second reading of the book, they were really upset as to why the characters were placed in the Big Box. They expressed feelings of anger at the parents and other adults who were responsible and were genuinely puzzled as to what regarding the children's behaviors led their parents to believe that they couldn't handle their freedom. They expressed concern with some adults and institutions that do not allow people to be themselves but realized that when someone is different they are sometimes picked on and in a sense "boxed."*

The notion of being "boxed" or "othered" led Janice's students to consider what boxes meant in their own lives. They made statements such as "The box is a place to put a problem so you don't have to deal with it" and "It is a mental [in your head] place rather than a physical place." The "box" they most identified with was being misunderstood by other students or by adults. In order to make further sense of their discussions, Janice asked her students to write about their thoughts regarding the book and the notion of being boxed. Her students commented that writing their thoughts helped them to organize their thinking about the text. It seemed writing was a way for Janice's students to think critically about *The Big Box*. While talking about his writing, Kyle described the box as a mental prison. He said, "It doesn't really exist. The parents made the big box up to trap the kids. And if it was real, it works like a playpen. It traps the kids inside, but the parents, teachers, etc., have complete access to them."

Liane connected with being boxed in as a result of being labeled gifted. She reflected,

> The other time I've been in a box was when my old friends officially knew I was gifted and they made something up called Liane Carrabanna. They said this character went to St. Rose and they hated her. It was very weird because they were always telling me about her, so I suspected something. I knew it was me. I was right. It was me. It was okay at first, but then I asked them why. They said they did it because I was too smart for them. I think the one way everyone puts everyone else in a box is when we don't give them chances and choices.

Katherine connected to having been boxed in as a result of being female:

> I've been put in a box a couple of times in my life, like when I get grounded. When people (especially boys my age or a bit older) say I'm substitute in a soccer game, or I'm sitting on the bench for the whole game because I'm "only a girl" because they (the team) don't need a girl.

After listening to her students' responses and reflecting on her own journal entries, Janice revisited her concern regarding their initial reaction to the book. She said, "Looking back, it seems to me that they needed to have some fun with the book to offset the intensity of their reactions."

*Reflection Point 4.3*_____

Think back to a time when you felt your students responded
strangely to a text you had read to them or a time when they responded in a way you had not anticipated. What did you do?
How did you react? Jot down a few things that you might have
done differently if given an opportunity.

_____

Until Janice talked further with her students, she had not considered
the multiplicity of issues regarding gender equity, fairness, and social justice
that her students were mulling over in their minds. It was not until she
read their writing and listened to their responses that she began to recognize these issues as important ones to take up in the classroom. Like Susan,
Janice was not prepared for how her students might react to tensions that
were clearly new to them. However, both realized that reading and responding critically could not be a one-time experience. As each of them
dealt with the social issues that began to surface in their own settings, they
noticed other issues beginning to emerge. For example, in Katherine's writing about *The Big Box*, it became clear to Janice that gender equity was an issue that she ought to take up in the classroom. In Susan's class, the issue
of white privilege emerged as her students raised concern over why some
white characters in *White Wash* "just watched" without consequence as
young Helene-Angel's face was painted white. The important lesson to be
gained from this chapter, therefore, is that there is no one-size-fits-all critical literacy, and that we need to construct different critical literacies depending on what work needs to be done in certain settings, contexts, or
communities, and that it needs to be negotiated using the cultural and linguistic resources to which children have had access.

In the next chapter, you will continue to hear about other ways of taking up critical literacies in the classroom. This time the focus is on using
children's literature in the content areas, specifically mathematics, to engage in a social action project.

Chapter 5

Integrating Critical Literacy, Children's Literature, and Mathematics Investigations

Teacher:	*You're not excited about the choices I mentioned this morning? (museum, zoo)*
Malcom:	*No. We've done those before. It's the same thing every year.*
Teacher:	*Hmm. I guess I never thought about it that way. Do you have any suggestions about where we might go?*
Malcom:	*I just think we should do something fun like a pool party or something.*
Teacher:	*Well, I'm pretty sure that because of rules the school board has in place that we can't do a pool party. They have concerns about students and safety.*
Georgia:	*Well, what if we didn't leave and had a day where we had a dance and pizza and then a party here in the room.*
Teacher:	*OK. That's an idea. Are there any others?*
Malcom:	*I think we should go to Canada's Wonderland [amusement theme park].*
Class:	*Yeah! That's a great idea!*

Mike Muise had just begun to explore opportunities for critical literacy with his fifth- and sixth-grade students when the previous conversation took place regarding an end-of-the-year class excursion. Mike's multiage classroom was in an urban elementary school in Toronto, Ontario, Canada. In this chapter you will become privy to the ways in which Mike and his students attempted to understand particular school institutional discourse in order to find the best way to advance their agenda of planning an alternative end-of-the-year celebration. Mike will share the use of children's literature and math investigations that resulted in creating space to encourage the critical reading of social practices within his own classroom. Social practices are ways of doing things within different social spaces and contexts.

Imagining What If...

Mike: *Sarah Perry's book* If... *(1995) entices readers to imagine what if.... What if worms had wheels? What if spiders could read Braille? or What if hummingbirds told secrets? Her book bends the imagination in much the same way a thick piece of glass refracts light, causing one's eyes to see something from a different perspective. I decided to read the book to my fifth and sixth graders. My intent was to use it as a way to generate writing and to inject some creativity and interest in my writing program. I envisioned it to be a way of stretching and pulling at my students' imagination. In the midst of a class discussion about the book, Malcolm asked, "What if we got to pick where we went for our end-of-the-year trip?"*

It was early May, and Mike and his students had been talking in class about where they might go for their end-of-the-year outing. He had provided his students with a number of choices including places other classes had visited in the past. The concept of choice, however, was not always clear to Mike.

Mike: *I recall trying to reason with my 3-year-old son, Avery, one evening around bath time. I informed him that he had three choices: (1) Get in the tub, (2) Get in bed, or (3) Get your mother. He responded, "But daddy, those aren't my choices. Those are yours." Malcolm, like Avery, was letting me know that my choices were just that—my choices. None of which were my students' choices. Clearly, my ideas for a school excursion were not what Malcolm or his classmates had in mind.*

Malcolm:	Are all school trips supposed to be no fun?
Teacher:	Well, not exactly, but we do need to let your parents and Mr. Morely [the school principal] know that our trip is tied to what we learned here in class.

Picking up on the what-if theme in the book they had been reading, Mike put forth the question, What if we were to think about our school trip from a mathematics perspective? J.J. responded, "Yeah. We could count the number of people in line-ups, and how much it costs for lunch, and...." It was then that Mike realized how he and his students might be able to use their proposed trip to Canada's Wonderland as a way to show administration and parents how mathematics is used in everyday contexts.

Mike: *Perry's book* If... *led to conversations that helped me to realize the choices I had been providing my students, although well intentioned, were in fact not their choices at all.*

Conversation about the book provided a forum for my students to examine everyday school practices such as the policy involved with approving or disapproving school events. In addition, discussion of texts such as If... *afforded me an opportunity to critically examine my teaching practices.*

Mike and his students had predicted that if they could connect the paper curriculum, in particular, the math curriculum that was mandated by the school board, to their proposed school trip to Canada's Wonderland, they would have a better chance of getting their trip approved by the school's administration. To do this, Mike implemented the use of math investigation journals (Schmidt, 1998). These were notebooks specifically used to write and think about mathematics-related topics, inquiry questions, and issues. They served as a tool for children to help sort through concepts they know or wish to know regarding mathematics. Mike and his students used the journal entries to develop topics for investigation. The process begins with a student selecting a topic of interest. Mike's students were interested in demonstrating to their parents and the school administrators the academic viability of a trip to Canada's Wonderland. Before beginning their research, Mike had his students map out a plan for their investigation and identify the resources they would be using.

Counting on Frank: Using Math Journals to Produce Data

To get the math investigations started, Mike decided to read to the class *Counting on Frank* by Rod Clement (1991). In this story, Frank, an inquisitive young boy, finds many uses for his talent of counting. He reveals an uncanny ability to use mathematics to estimate, hypothesize, and theorize about the world around him:

> My dad says, "You have a brain. Use it!" So I do. I sit down and fill my notebook with facts. Did you know that the average ballpoint pen draws a line 7,000 feet long before the ink runs out? My parents consider this fact to be a bit childish, but I'm sure the pen company would like to know. (n.p.)

Mike used the book to set up a discussion for his students to identify math unfolding in the world. Mike realized the potential for taking up other social issues with the book including gender equity. For the time being, however, he decided to focus on the Canada's Wonderland project.

Mike asked his students to brainstorm ways in which mathematics was used at Canada's Wonderland. This initiating experience led his students to generate some ideas about where mathematics was used in the daily functioning of the theme park. Each student was then provided with a math investigation journal in which to record thoughts, findings, comments, and questions. (See Figure 8 for examples of the children's work.)

Reflection Point 5.1

Make a list of the last five books you read to or with your class.

1. For each book, identify what you did with the book.

2. What kind of work did you hope to accomplish?

3. For what area of the curriculum was each book used?

4. What are some ways that you might use books written for children alongside other everyday texts to set up particular discussions in the content areas?

Figure 8
Examples of Children's Work in Their Math Journals

I learned that in order to build roller coasters builders must use geometry, and measurement to construct the ride. Right angles 90°, 45° and other angles.

(continued)

Figure 8 (continued)
Examples of Children's Work in Their Math Journals

In order for Canada's Wonderland to run as a business they have to take people's money. Money is used so that people can get into the park, buy food and even play games.

(continued)

Figure 8 (continued)
Examples of Children's Work in Their Math Journals

In his own journal, Mike wrote,

> I witnessed my students engaged in learning at many levels. Many logged onto the computer searching for websites that could inform their research. Some discovered the role of angles, measurement, time, and velocity in the construction of park rides such as roller coasters. Other students buried themselves in the library, searching out books that explored other theme parks around the world, trying to gather data on such things as park capacities, ride capacities, and group discounts. Others looked at maps of Toronto to identify the quickest and most cost efficient route to Wonderland from our school.

Mike: *Our classroom engagements around their goal of going to Canada's Wonderland lasted approximately two weeks. As a culminating experience, the students agreed that a letter to the school principal would be appropriate. It was discussed that before we sought permission from parents we should get approval from the school. With this in mind, each student was asked to draft a letter demonstrating what he or she had learned with regard to mathematical uses at an amusement park.*

Throughout the following week, the students engaged in formulating a class letter that accompanied their individual letters.

> Dear Mr. Morley,
>
> For the past several weeks, Mr. Muise's class has been working very hard to demonstrate to you and the parents that a class trip to Canada's Wonderland would not only be a tremendous amount of fun but also would be a very good educational experience.
>
> In order to support our argument, we decided to explore the many uses of mathematics within the everyday operations of Canada's Wonderland. In our research, which lasted more then two weeks, we discovered that in order for this park to function they have to make use of geometry, currency, time, fractions, division, multiplication, addition, subtraction, probability, velocity, problem solving, and measurement. These are all areas of math that we have looked at this year and in the past.
>
> We feel that we have worked very hard to find several reasons why this trip would be educational. Please consider our trip to Canada's Wonderland. It is something that we all want very badly. We have attached a few of our math investigation journals for you to look at. We hope you will see that we have done a lot of work to show you that this trip would be both educational and safe. We think it would be a lot of fun too.
>
> Sincerely,
> Mr. Muise's Grade 5–6 Students

The letter was submitted to the school's principal on a Tuesday afternoon. On Wednesday morning before the children arrived at school, Mike was called into Mr. Morley's office. Mr. Morley wanted to know what the letter was all about. Mike informed him that he had provided the children with the opportunity to choose where they would go for their end-of-year excursion and that the class unanimously decided on a visit to Canada's Wonderland. Mike reassured him that he understood his concerns and shared with him the children's research on the educational value of such a trip.

Mike: *I asked him if he had read the letter and the math investigation journals the kids had completed. He responded that he, in fact, had looked them over and, while he did find them to be most impressive he was unsure how the school board would feel about a group of 10- to 12-year olds going to an amusement park. He informed me that in all likelihood he would have to say no to the class's proposal. I asked him how he planned to let them know that their efforts were fruitless. He asked if I would let them know. I responded by asking him to come to the class and let them know himself. We compromised with a letter from his office.*

In his letter to Mike's students, Mr. Morley wrote,

> Dear Mr. Muise's Grade 5–6 Students,
>
> I want to thank you for your letter requesting permission to go to Canada's Wonderland for your end-of-the-school-year trip. It is clear to me that you all have done a tremendous amount of work. I am impressed that you have found so many practical uses for mathematics within the everyday workings of Canada's Wonderland. However, it is unlikely that such a trip would receive school board approval. There are guidelines and regulations that teachers and principals must abide by when considering places to visit for school outings. My main concern arises around the theme park's water rides. There are very strict rules about students participating in any engagements outside of school that involve water. I am sure you will understand that this decision was not an easy one. I appreciate your incredible work efforts.
>
> Sincerely,
> Mr. Morley

It should come as no surprise that Mike's class was disappointed. As he read the letter to them, their shoulders fell and their faces expressed disappointment. Numerous sighs and moans could be heard. Malcolm, however, spoke up and asked, "Who makes the rules for teachers anyway?" Mike told him that many people are involved in creating the rules that are meant to ensure students' time in school is safe and educational. He alluded, however, to the school board as being the primary constructors of such rules. Malcolm then asked who could be contacted at the school board so that he and some others from the class could show how much work had been done in preparation for the proposed trip. Mike told his students that if they wanted to contact someone, the superintendent would be the next logical person. With Malcolm's encouragement, the class decided that a letter should be sent to the superintendent asking for his permission to go to Canada's Wonderland. Over the course of the next few days, the students drafted, edited, revised, and rewrote potential letters to the school superintendent. Following is the letter the children decided to send.

> Dear Mr. Owen,
>
> For the past several weeks, we have been researching the many uses of math within the everyday functioning of Canada's Wonderland. It is our hope that in doing so you will be able to see that such a trip would not only be a tremendous amount of fun, but would also be educational. We sent a letter to Mr. Morley in hope that he would approve our trip, but he said that the rules in place would make it very difficult for him to do so. We are hoping that you can help us in our hope of going to Canada's Wonderland for our end-of-the-year school trip. We have enclosed copies of our math investigation journals in which we did all of our research. You will see that we have found many everyday uses of mathematics at Canada's Wonderland.
>
> Sincerely,
> Mr. Muise's Grade 5–6 Students

Reflection Point 5.2

Make a list of the various ways that you have used writing in your curriculum. How have you used writing as a response to books? What are some other ways that you might use writing in your classroom as a way for your students to act on issues that matter to them?

Mike: *Unfortunately, our class never did hear back from the superinten-dent. We did inquire further with Mr. Morley, however, who continued to say that without the school board's approval he would not be able to grant us per-mission to go on a trip to Canada's Wonderland.*

For the most part, the parents were completely supportive of the chil-dren's wishes for their trip. When Mike asked what convinced them such a trip would be a good thing, many of the parents pointed to the math investigation journals as viable data that demonstrated the children had grown academically. Although they were unable to fulfill their hopes of going to Canada's Wonderland, Mike felt it was one of the most exciting experiences for both him and his students.

Using Children's Literature to Create Spaces for Critically Reading Classroom Practice

In spite of the fact that the letter writing and research failed to bring about desired results, Mike was pleased to have had the opportunity for his stu-dents to examine the everyday uses of math. In addition, and perhaps more important, they had an opportunity and willingness to act on what they believed. Their initiating experience, born out of Malcolm's response to the book *If...*, provided an opportunity to critically examine existing school prac-tices. From Mike's vantage point, discussions that resulted from reading the book provided his students with the what-if metaphor, creating a forum through which his own shortcomings as an educator became visible to him.

Mike: *Before the discussions that followed our reading* If..., *I believed that by providing my students with choices I was able to support my quest for democracy within my classroom. What I was failing to see was how my choic-es were limiting rather than generative.*

Reflection Point 5.3

Reflect on the kinds of choices you make available in your class-room. How might you negotiate choices that take into account issues that are important to your students?

Through the exchange of letters, Mike and his students discovered the decisions about the kind of knowledge that counts in schools are made not only by students and teachers but also by the school administrators. Even though the children in his class had worked diligently researching practical everyday uses of mathematics convincing school administration that such knowledge is viable and valuable, school board officials ultimately make decisions as to the kind of knowledge that should be valued in classrooms.

Regardless, Mike and his students learned a great deal. His students challenged him to examine how he was attempting to create a democratic classroom and where he was failing to do so. As a community, the students discovered that not everything is distributed equally. Most important, they discovered that power is unequally distributed within the school system. They learned that those in positions outside the classroom value particular kinds of knowledge. They decided, however, that they had ways and opportunities to question all that had been put in place by those outside the classroom. Malcolm had this to say as a result of asking, What if?: "I have learned more from planning this trip than any other even if we didn't get to go!"

Chapter 6

New Directions and Curricular Possibilities for Doing "Important Work"

Teacher:	*I can't believe that it's already June.*
Patricia:	*Yeah. September, October, November...June.*
Alexandro:	*Lots of months, lots of learning.*
Emma:	*And lots of books. I like books.*
Alexandro:	*Yes...books and more books.*
Teacher:	*What are some things you've learned about books this year?*
Alexandro:	*When we talked about books, mostly we talked about us.*
Teacher:	*Tell me more about that.*
Emma:	*Not just words, right?*
Patricia:	*Right. Mostly our talk and using words and pictures to do work like changing what's not fair.*
Alexandro:	*Sometimes that's hard, but sometimes not so hard.*
Patricia:	*But that's important work, right Emma?*
Emma:	*Right Patricia.*

It is the end of the school year. My (Vivian's) kindergarten students who you met at the beginning of this book sat informally chatting about the year that had passed. Their talk focused on their work with books and how that work was sometimes hard and sometimes not so hard, but most important they understood they had done important work to change "what's not fair."

The "important work" that Patricia and Emma referred to in this exchange includes the experiences we had with all sorts of texts—using texts not just for pleasure or enjoyment but also to create spaces for understanding how language works to construct people, for using language to critique the word and the world, and for changing social practices that advantage some people over others. By adopting a critical pedagogy that made it possible for my students and me to investigate the positions taken up by texts, I was able to help my students become literate beings who question things that are taken for granted or are assumed to be normal or natural in the world (see Box 6.1 for resources on critical literacy in practice). My students and I did this by critically reading and analyzing the world in which we live. We analyzed the things with which we agreed and disagreed.

Reflection Point 6.1

1. Reflect on what might be made possible by adopting a critical pedagogy in your setting.

2. What are some theoretical and practical notions about critical literacy that you learned from this book?

If you recall, I opened this book with a conversation between Patricia and Alexandro regarding their disappointment in discovering that there were no books about the Philippines in our school library even though there were large numbers of Filipino students in our school. Their concern was mainly for their new classmate, Emma, who had just arrived from the Philippines. Therefore, it is ironic to notice that in the previous conversation it was Emma who noted that books are "not just words right?"

My collaborators in this book share Emma's sentiments that books and other texts are "not just words." In each of their classrooms, books were more than tools for learning language and learning about language. They used books as one of several tools for using language to critique, and in so doing, to question, interrogate, problematize, denaturalize, interrupt, and disrupt that which appears normal, natural, ordinary, mundane, and

---

Box 6.1
Resources on Critical Literacy in Practice

Comber, B., & Simpson, A. (2001). *Negotiating critical literacies in classrooms*. Mahwah, NJ: Erlbaum.

Comber, B., & Thomson, P., with Wells, M. (2001). Critical literacy finds a "place": Writing and social action in a neighborhood school. *The Elementary School Journal, 101*(4), 451–464.

Edelsky, C. (Ed.). (2000). *Making justice our project*. Urbana, IL: National Council of Teachers of English.

Fehring, H., & Green, P. (Eds.). (2001). *Critical literacy: A collection of articles from the Australian Literacy Educators' Association*. Newark, DE: International Reading Association.

Heffernan, L., & Lewison, M. (2000). Making real-world issues our business: Critical literacy in a third-grade classroom. *Primary Voices K–6, 9*(2), 15–21.

Marsh, J. (2000). "But I want to fly too!": Girls and superhero play in the infant classroom. *Gender and Education, 12*(2), 209–220.

Mellor, B., O'Neill, M., & Patterson, A. (2000). *Reading stories: Activities and texts for critical readings*. Urbana, IL: National Council of Teachers of English.

Morgan, W. (1997). *Critical literacy in the classroom*. New York: Routledge.

Muspratt, S., Luke, A., & Freebody, P. (1997). *Constructing critical literacies: Teaching and learning textual practice*. Cresskill, NJ: Hampton Press.

O'Brien, J. (1994). Show Mum you love her: Taking a new look at junk mail. *Reading, 28*(1), 43–46.

Vasquez, V. (1998). Building equitable communities: Taking social action in a kindergarten classroom. *Talking Points, 9*(2), 3–6.

Vasquez, V. (2000). Building community through social action. *School Talk, 5*(4), 2–3.

Vasquez, V. (2000). Language stories and critical literacy lessons. *Talking Points, 11*(2), 5–7.

Vasquez, V. (2000). Our way: Using the everyday to create a critical literacy curriculum. *Primary Voices, 9*(2), 8–13.

Vasquez, V. (2003). *Negotiating critical literacy with young children*. Mahwah, NJ: Erlbaum

---

everyday, as well as to redesign, reconstruct, reimagine, rethink, and reconsider social worlds, spaces, and places. Using language to critique helped each of us to understand that books and other texts, including multimedia texts, are ideological sites or spaces for systemic values to reside. Together we grew to understand that the point of reading the "word" and the "world" against the grain such as discussing various issues from different perspectives is to help illuminate particular topics associated with power and control such as racism and gender inequity in order to create spaces to take action in and on the world.

My collaborators and I were at different places in our conceptualization of critical literacy as we created this book. Given a different time and space, we each could have told different stories, moved in different directions, and worked with different texts to practice the use of language in more powerful ways. One common denominator in each of our stories, however, is that all of us attempted to create spaces in our particular locations to engage in the "important work" referred to by Patricia and Emma. We hope that this book helps you to do the same.

Reflection Point 6.2

Review your responses to the Reflection Points in this book.

1. What insights have you gained about critical literacy?

2. What have you learned about using books written for children as one tool for taking up critical conversations and social action with children?

3. How might you create spaces for critical literacy in your classroom?

Getting Started

Through writing different accounts of working with books in K–6 classrooms, my collaborators and I intended to share not only our successes and pleasures, but also our tensions. I hope our stops and starts were visible to you as you read through the pages of this book, and that reflecting on our work provided you with a space for thinking about ways of working critically with books written for children, as well as other texts. The instances of learning presented in the previous pages were not meant as definitive answers for "doing" critical literacy using children's books. Rather, they were examples of attempts at finding spaces for critical literacies through using children's books as one way to begin to make accessible to students a metalanguage to challenge the potential of texts to impose limited ways of thinking about the world. I hope that the different accounts of critical work with books and other texts provide you with opportunities to think differently about the role that children's literature can play in a classroom, and that you are able to find space to begin engaging in critical literacies.

Appendix A

Books Written for Young People by Young People

Although the children's book market has been supported by adult authors, child authors have contributed to the market as well. For example, S.E. Hinton began writing *The Outsiders* at age 15. The book was published in 1967 and has sold more than one million copies.

Anne Frank's diary was published in English in 1952 as *The Diary of a Young Girl*. Anne wrote the book as a teenager, describing her family's life in hiding during World War II when Jews were being persecuted. It has been translated into more than 50 languages.

At age 12, Ally Sheedy wrote *She Was Nice to Mice*; it was published in 1975. It is the story of a mouse taken back in time through her family history to the days of Queen Elizabeth I and William Shakespeare.

More recently, more child authors have begun to have their work published. Following is a list of some of these works, including a reprint edition of S.E. Hinton's *The Outsiders*.

Dewitt, J. (1987). *Jamie's turn*. Chicago: Raintree.

Gac-Artigas, A. (2001). *Yo Alejandro* (2nd English ed.). Fairview, NJ: Ediciones Nuevo Espacio.

Gaes, J. (1987). *My book for kids with cansur: A child's autobiography of hope*. Aberdeen, SD: Melius.

Hinton, S.E. (1997). *The Outsiders* (Reprint ed.). White Plains, NY: Prentice Hall.

Klein, D.J. (1987). *Irwin the sock*. Chicago: Raintree.

Lebert, B. (2001). *Crazy*. Vancouver, WA: Vintage International.

Meyer, S.H., & Meyer, J. (Eds). (2001). *Teen ink: Friends and family*. Newton, MA: The Young Authors Foundation.

Tamaki, M. (2000). *Cover me*. Toronto: McGilligan Books.

Appendix B

Annotated Bibliography of Books That Explore Social Issues

Compiled by Lee Heffernan

Blumberg, R. (1996). *Bloomers*. New York: Aladdin.

> The early history of the women's rights movement is traced through the story of Amelia Bloomer and the pants she invented for women. Amelia is most famous for the pants that were named after her, but she also ran a newspaper, *The Lily*, and was active in the suffragette movement.
>
> The author gives examples of how confining and potentially dangerous women's clothing could be. When a woman walked upstairs, she had to lift her long dress. If she were carrying a child and a candle at the same time, she not only had difficulty moving, but she also put herself and the child in danger. This type of detail from daily life makes the hardships of living in a sexist society more real for readers. Gender roles and fashion rules are topics for conversation as readers discover that restrictions placed on dress have a historical context that still affects society today.

Bunting, E. (1998). *Your Move*. Ill. J. Ransome. New York: Harcourt Brace.

> James is 10 and his 6-year-old brother Isaac likes to imitate him. One evening after their mother goes to work, James sneaks out to meet the K-Bones and takes Isaac with him because he can't leave his little brother home alone. The K-Bones, led by Kris and Bones, aren't a gang or a crew; they say they are just guys who hang out together. James thinks he wants to join them, so they give him a task—spray paint the K-Bones' name over the Snakes' name on a sign over the highway.

77

In the end, Isaac ends up with two skinned knees, but *Your Move* does much more than scratch the surface of issues connected to gang violence and peer pressure. Bunting explores the reasons why James and Isaac are attracted to the K-Bones. The reasons they both decide not to join the K-Bones when offered the chance are even more compelling. Critical discussion could begin with the choices James and Isaac make. What attracts them to the K-Bones? Why do they decide not to join? Are there differences in the ways James and Isaac make their decisions? Exploring with students what they think is important and how they have faced or would face similar decisions is crucial, especially because even very young children often need to make difficult and important decisions.

Coerr, E. (1979). *Sadako and the Thousand Paper Cranes*. New York: Yearling.

The story of Sadako, a young girl who died of leukemia after the U.S. bombing of Hiroshima and Nagasaki, has become almost mythic in U.S. schools. Origami cranes can be seen hanging in classrooms of all grade levels as symbols of peace. The details of Sadako's life, however, are still eye-opening to readers. In this short chapter book, Coerr details the anguish of postwar Japanese citizens who live in fear of contracting the atom bomb disease years after the bombing.

The sadness of this story is often surprising to young readers, who have a hard time dealing with stories that don't end happily—as stories for young children often do. Readers gain a real understanding of the long-term consequences of military intervention around the world today. Issues of innocence and guilt can apply to a number of historical and present-day situations.

Hesse, K. (1996). *Music of Dolphins*. New York: Scholastic.

A feral child is found living with dolphins in the sea near a Caribbean island. She is transported to Boston where she becomes the subject of a series of psychological studies. She is trusting and eager at the outset, but eventually shuts down emotionally as she comes to understand that she is essentially a prisoner.

The social scientist in charge of Mila depends on the government for funding of her work. This dependence creates a dilemma for her because conducting her experiments interferes with the well-being of her subject. This book prompts talk about personal freedom, ethical scientific method, language, and learning.

The format of the book is intriguing. The font size is extra large in the beginning chapters when the main character knows little English. As she learns and develops her language and social skills, the font size is gradually reduced.

McCully, E.A. (1996). *The Bobbin Girl*. New York: Dial.

Rebecca Putney is a 10-year-old bobbin girl in 19th-century Lowell, Massachusetts. She works 13-hour days in unhealthy working conditions in order to help support her family. The story, however, is not as much about Rebecca as it is about the social and industrial milieu of the times. More specifically, the story provides much-needed space in which to encourage conversation about issues of child labor and child abuse as well as issues of labor control, enslavement, and the marginalization of women. In the story, Rebecca befriends Judith, another mill worker, who puts up with the conditions at the mill in order to finance her studies. It is Judith who rises to the occasion, standing up for the rights of the female factory workers when the mill owner decides to reduce already low wages. At first it appears that the female workers may stand united against management, but in the end many of them abandon the protest and return to work, driven by the illusion that working in the mill represents their independence.

The Bobbin Girl does not explicitly present itself as a story of triumph for women. However, it does raise a number of questions regarding the difficulties involved in any struggle for equity and social justice. It also points to the need for ongoing social action. With regard to gender issues, the book easily lends itself to discussions of what happens when women break with convention and move into positions that challenge the ingrained gender biases in our society.

McCully's use of a dark palette and shadows effectively conveys the feeling of the poor conditions in the mill.

McGuffee, M. (1996). *The Day the Earth Was Silent*. Ill. E. Sullivan. Bloomington, IN: Inquiring Voices Press.

A classroom of students makes a beautiful new flag that they want to share with all the earth. The principal asks, "Why try?" But one student insists, "Why not try?" So the principal tells the students to ask the mayor for help. This exchange goes through several permutations as the children keep asking and keep hearing from weary adults all the reasons for giving up their plan—it involves too much work, it's too expensive, and so on. Finally, at a meeting of all the nations, the students unveil their flag, and the people of earth finally see—Why not!

This isn't simply a story of visionary optimism; it's also about the importance of persistence and cherishing small yet significant moments of social change. Edward Sullivan's illustrations brightly radiate the energy of students engaged in creative expression and social action. Possible conversations abound on the potential of imagining, creating, questioning, and working together (not to mention listening to children) to change our world for the better. And, what better way for the conversation to continue than when children choose and implement their own dreams to share with their community and world.

Mochizuki, K. (1997). *Passage to Freedom: The Sugihara Story*. Ill. D. Lee. New York: Lee & Low.

In July 1940, young Hiroki Sugihara, son of the Japanese consul to Lithuania, saw hundreds of Jewish refugees from Poland gathered at the gate of his family home. These refugees wanted travel visas so that they could escape imminent persecution. After Consul Sugihara is denied government permission to grant the visas, he asks his family if he should write the visas anyway, risking the consequences. While Consul Sugihara hand writes thousands of visas, Hiroki plays with the refugee children in the park. When the Soviets take over Lithuania, they order Consul Sugihara to leave, just as the Japanese government reassigns him to Germany. But, as the fascinating afterword notes, thousands of refugees are saved.

Dom Lee's sepia-toned illustrations beautifully convey the intense emotion of the Sugihara and refugee families, although they are also reminiscent of stark, black-and-white holocaust photos. This story will raise important conversations about human rights; the relationships among compassion, courage, and sacrifice; nonviolent resistance; and the power of the pen as an instrument of social justice.

Yamate, S. (1992). *Ashok by Any Other Name*. Chicago: Polychrome Publications.

> Ashok, an American boy whose parents are from India, gets fed up when his name is mispronounced at school year after year. He changes his name several times, resulting in some predictable problems. Only when the librarian, an African American teacher, talks to him about how his ancestors were robbed of their nomenclature does Ashok come to appreciate his name as a symbol of his cultural identity.
>
> Although Ashok's problem initially seems insignificant to readers, he is able to make the choice to change his name or retain it. This book leads students to share stories about how their names have sometimes created problems for them at school.

Appendix C

Annotated Bibliography of Books That Depict Social Action

Bartoletti, S. (1999). *Kids on Strike!* Boston: Houghton Mifflin.

Bartoletti's historical account of children in the workforce is complemented by hundreds of authentic, gripping photographs of children at work on city streets, in coal mines, and in the garment industry. The images of the children and descriptions of their inhumane working conditions provide opportunities to raise questions about human nature, progress, U.S. economic values, and the corporate agenda. The author highlights the resiliency and collective power of children by recounting the ways in which children have participated in acts of resistance and organized strikes. The book also raises issues about how effective children's efforts were in changing their own lives, how children's limited powers compare to the power of others to silence and control them in the pursuit of wealth and progress, and others who are disadvantaged in society.

Breckler, R. (1996). *Sweet Dried Apples: A Vietnamese Wartime Childhood*. Ill. D.K. Ray. Boston: Houghton Mifflin.

This story is told from the viewpoint of a young Vietnamese girl whose life is changed by the encroaching war that comes to encompass her family and her life. The girl's grandfather, Ong Noi, is a "revered elder" who has been the herb doctor in his village for many years. When his son becomes a soldier, Ong Noi comes to help look after his two grandchildren. Ong Noi brings baskets of medicinal herbs and sweet dried apples to cover their bitter taste. When Ong Noi leaves to tend wounded soldiers in a distant area, the grandchildren continue to gather herbs as he taught them to do. In the end, Ong Noi sacrifices his own life so that others can have relief from pain and suffering. He gives all his medicines to others and saves nothing to heal his own wounds. This book invites conversations about the different forms that social action can take and how this action affects people's lives.

Brumbeau, J. (2000). *The Quilt Maker's Gift*. Ill. G. de Marcken. New York: Scholastic.

This book is a story about a generous quilt maker "with magic in her fingers" and a greedy king with "his storehouse stuffed with treasures." The quilt maker sews the most beautiful quilts in the world to give to the poor and needy. The king, in spite of his riches, yearns for something that he believes will make him happy—a quilt. However, the quilt maker refuses to make one for him, saying she will only do so if he gives away all his possessions. In the end, the king gives away his treasures and, in so doing, learns this lesson from the quilt maker: True happiness comes not from material possessions, but in letting them go to bring happiness to others. Through taking social action to support others, the king finally finds happiness.

Cronin, D. (2000). *Click, Clack, Moo: Cows That Type*. Ill. B. Lewin. New York: Simon & Schuster.

Farmer Brown has a problem. His cows have found an old typewriter in the barn and are using it to make demands. They want electric blankets to keep them warm at night and are willing to withhold their milk until they get them. What is worse, the chickens have joined the cows in their strike. No more milk! No more eggs! The ducks are the not-so-neutral party. They carry the cows' and chickens' message, which promises to turn over the typewriter in exchange for blankets. Once Farmer Brown capitulates, however, the animals have a few new demands of their own. The delightfully understated text and expressive illustrations add to the hilarity. A read-aloud must for teachers who wish to create space in their classroom for conversations about literacy and power with even the youngest of readers.

Dash, J. (1996). *We Shall Not Be Moved: The Women's Factory Strike of 1909*. New York: Scholastic.

This historical account of the events leading up to a massive women's factory strike almost a century ago shows how taking social action and working together can help to improve conditions for those who lack power. In this case, three groups took part in social action. The first group, the "shirtwaist" factory workers, mostly poor young women between the ages of 16 and 18, had the courage to stand up to the powerful factory owners and demand better pay and better working conditions. Starving and without warm clothing, they picketed in the cold and continued their strike for months. When they were terrorized and brutally beaten by hired guerillas and hauled off to jail by corrupt police, two other groups of women became involved: "The mink brigade" (wealthy women) and "the college girls" had power and were ready to use it to fight for their progressive beliefs. When the strike ended, conditions for the factory workers had improved only slightly, but other gains had been made in terms of raising the public consciousness and the acceptance of a labor union that would ultimately protect the workers who followed.

Fradin, D., & Fradin, J. (2001). *Ida B. Wells: Mother of the Civil Rights Movement*. New York: Clarion Books.

This book is a historical account of Ida B. Wells, who championed voting rights for women, spoke out against lynching, and helped to establish the National Association for the Advancement of Colored People (NAACP). The book shares her life story as she crusaded against the unlawful treatment of African Americans in the early part of the 20th century.

Outspoken in her beliefs, Wells did not hesitate to make it known that she believed that those who did nothing to stop lynching and discrimination were just as guilty as those who had committed those injustices. Wells was one of the most vocal protesters of her time and later became the spiritual mother of the U.S. Civil Rights movement. Throughout the chapters, there are striking photographs of Wells, her family, her colleagues; pamphlets and other writings; and the horrors of lynching.

The book provides an opportunity for readers to engage in important conversations about social action and how we all have the potential to make a difference.

Hansen, J. (1998). *Women of Hope: African Americans Who Made a Difference*. New York: Scholastic Press.

> A teacher for 22 years in New York City, Hansen describes her combined message of self-empowerment and community service in this way: "By reaching their goals, these women helped someone else." Hansen's page-length, chronologically arranged inspiring biographies depict the lives of 13 African American women. We meet celebrity authors Maya Angelou and Toni Morrison; Ida Wells-Barnet, a teacher and journalist at the turn of the century who exposed inequities in education for black students and the brutality of lynching in the South; and Dr. Mae C. Jemison, who was not only the first African American woman astronaut but who also worked as a physician in West Africa.
>
> The artists, educators, healthcare providers, and activists in these biographies provide role models and inspiration on many levels and in the integrity, passion, and struggle of their life work as well as in their own words. Students' critical questions could explore the obstacles that each of these women faced; the resources they called on to overcome them; and the ways they redefined cultural notions of courage, strength, and heroism. What is perhaps most important is how these biographies invite exploration of the unique and individual journeys each of us makes toward finding meaning in our lives.

Kaplan, W. (1998). *One More Border: The True Story of One Family's Escape From War-Torn Europe*. Ill. S. Taylor. Toronto: Groundwood Books.

> The story reveals the social repositioning of the Kaplan family from living in comfort and luxury to being penniless. It is thought-provoking in raising issues regarding how some cultural practices and traditions oppress certain groups or individuals. Questions that can be raised include, Who stands to gain from the oppression of others? What do they gain? What are some ways of interrogating persecution in order to take social action and effect change? When partnered with *Passage to Freedom: The Sugihara Story*, this text set offers a rich demonstration of how people taking social action can make a difference in the lives of the oppressed. Through the support of others, the Kaplans were able to position themselves differently, and readers are offered a glimpse of their new home in Cornwall, Ontario, Canada.

But not all Jewish families who experienced persecution were able to start anew as the Kaplans did. Thus, the book can generate further inquiries into what happened to those who were not able to escape. The book can also open up conversations regarding the different ways that some groups and individuals continue to be persecuted and oppressed.

McCully, E. (1998). *The Ballot Box Battle*. New York: Knopf.

The Ballot Box Battle, set in the late 1800s, is a weaving of history and fiction that shares the parallel stories of two females who challenge social norms and expectations. Cordelia is a young girl and a neighbor to suffragist Elizabeth Cady Stanton. As the book unfolds, we learn of Cordelia's desire to jump a four-foot fence on horseback, a feat that her brother is sure she cannot accomplish. Paralleled with Stanton's story of going to the polls to attempt to vote and fighting for women's suffrage, Cordelia's goal becomes insignificant when she accompanies Stanton to cast a ballot. However, the Stanton story is one that is not currently told or made visible in picture book form. As such, the book holds a place of importance as a demonstration of what it means to take up the plight of women as a marginalized group. The book also clearly reminds us of the position of men, especially white men, as dominant decision makers, thus opening up the possibility for a discussion of ways in which women can redefine their position in society.

Miller, W. (1998). *The Bus Ride*. Ill. John Ward. New York: Lee & Low.

"It's always been this way," Sara's mother replies when Sara asks why she and other African Americans have to ride in the back of the bus. Curious as to what could possibly justify such a law, Sara heads off to the front of the bus. Once up front, she takes a seat and realizes that the only difference is that white people sit there. Regardless, Sara decides to take a seat.

Based on the Montgomery, Alabama, bus boycott and framed through the experience of Rosa Parks, *The Bus Ride* can be used as a vehicle through which to have conversations about how certain groups of people are marginalized by some cultural practices and traditions. Questions can be raised such as, Who does the law support?

and Who benefits most from certain laws? The story also opens space to talk about the role the media can play in raising consciousness or maintaining inequities. Most important, *The Bus Ride* offers a demonstration of possibility for effecting social change through taking action as individuals or groups.

Ringgold, F. (1999). *If a Bus Could Talk: The Story of Rosa Parks*. New York: Simon & Schuster.

Author Faith Ringgold uses brilliant acrylic illustrations and a magical realist plot to tell the story of Rosa Parks. From the moment when Marcie, a young African American girl, steps onto the strange, driverless bus, readers learn about the events in the life of Parks told from the voices of famous passengers—all of whom participated in the Montgomery, Alabama, bus boycott. Although criticized for its condensed form, there is a remarkable amount of information about Parks presented in this picture book format. She is portrayed as a courageous political activist, and readers discover much about her life before and after the boycott. This book can open up conversations about the U.S. Civil Rights movement, segregation, and political activism.

Appendix D

Annotated Bibliography of Books for Creating Space to Talk About Issues of Racism, Power, and Control

Bunting, E. (1998). *So Far From the Sea*. Ill. C. Soentpiet. New York: Clarion Books.

> In 1942, the Japanese bombed Pearl Harbor; two months later, President Franklin D. Roosevelt signed Executive Order 9066 decreeing that all people of Japanese ancestry living on the west coast of the United States must be relocated to internment camps. Many of those interned were U.S. citizens.
>
> Set in 1972, *So Far From the Sea* is a story of the Iwaskaki family and their visit to the internment camp in California where their father was interned for $3^1/_2$ years. The story raises important issues about the segregation of the Japanese during the war and offers a demonstration of how easily people can be "othered." Questions regarding citizenry, who decides what makes a good citizen, and who qualifies to be one can be raised. The story allows space for conversations regarding segregation that exists today and the systems that maintain its existence.
>
> The illustrations by Soentpiet alternate between black-and-white and color, effectively supporting Bunting's description of the sensitive journey.

Coleman, E. (1996). *White Socks Only*. Ill. T. Geter. Morton Grove, IL: Albert Whitman.

> Inspired by childhood memories of places she could not go and things she could not do because of her skin color, Evelyn Coleman

presents a thought-provoking story that can provide much-needed conversations about segregation, marginalization, the inequitable distribution of power and control, as well as finding ways to take social action in what can appear to be the least likely places.

This is a story of a young African American girl who goes to town to fry an egg on the sidewalk and decides to take a drink from a water fountain in segregated Mississippi. Thinking that she understands the "Whites Only" sign on the fountain, she sits down in the grass, takes off her patent leather shoes, and climbs up on the stool to take a drink with only her clean white socks on her feet. When some of the town's white residents attempt to chastise and humiliate the child, her fellow African Americans who witnessed the event decide to take action.

The story ends with "And from then on, the 'Whites Only' sign was gone from that water fountain forever." The signs may be gone from water fountains, but issues of inequity continue to be played out across the United States. *White Socks Only* is a powerful source to generate conversations for interrogating such inequities.

Lester, J. (1998). *From Slave Ship to Freedom Road*. Ill. R. Brown. New York: Puffin.

Julius Lester describes the brutality of 300 years of the slave trade in this picture book, illustrated with the powerful paintings of Rod Brown. The story is presented through a combination of descriptive prose, imagination exercises, and first-person narrative, making for a unique read-aloud experience. Details of the horrors on the slave ships are disturbing for all readers, but this type of historical accuracy is missing from many picture books about slavery.

The author points out that, in addition to slave resistance, many white people fought against slavery as well. This book can be used as a springboard for digging deeper into some of the wide range of voices and perspectives presented in this text. This book is a powerful history lesson, but it also sparks conversation about our world today as readers of all ages become alerted to incidents of racism in the news and in daily life.

Loribiecki, M. (1996). *Just One Flick of a Finger*. Ill. David Diaz. New York: Dial.

> From the first stanza of this story poem, the reader is drawn into the urban tale of two boys trying to cope with the violence that handguns bring into their lives. The boys know well enough the dangers of handguns and can articulate the reasons not to use these weapons. Yet, when one of the boys feels threatened by an older peer, he decides to ignore his good sense and takes his father's gun to school. The handgun discharges accidentally wounding the boy and his friend. Although it is a hard lesson, the boy comes to see the folly of carrying a loaded handgun for "protection"and vows to rely on his friends and his own intellect to solve his problems in the future. Life in an urban setting is closely scrutinized in this story. The issues of handguns, personal responsibility, handling conflicts, and making choices can all be interrogated using the context of this story.
>
> The use of street language and rhyme gives the story the feel of a rap song. The author's choice to write this story in the form of a poem using urban dialect is both appropriate and intriguing. The illustrations are a combination of vivid background abstract drawings and individually framed pictures of the characters. The abstract background drawings look somewhat like graffiti, while the framed pictures are like snapshots that record the action as the story progresses. The use of bold colors in the artwork adds to the intense feelings and drama inherent in this all too realistic narrative.

Shange, N. (1997). *White Wash*. Ill. M. Sporn. New York: Walker.

> Helene-Angel, an African American preschooler, walks home from school with her brother, who doesn't particularly enjoy the task of walking his little sister home. One day a gang of white children surrounds them, blackening Mauricio's eye and painting Helene-Angel's face white as they show her how to be a"true American"and"how to be white." Helene-Angel is, of course, traumatized; she hides in her room until her grandmother encourages her to come out. As she emerges from the house, her classmates greet her and promise to stick together so that events like this won't happen again.

Based on a series of true incidents, *White Wash* is a powerful story written in narrative style by the poet Ntozaki Shange, with award-winning illustrations. Overall, the story gives voice to a little-known racial incident that becomes a lesson in tolerance and triumph. Children need to understand why such lessons should never be forgotten. They also should be encouraged to begin to explore how they might transform the bad things in their own lives into triumphs. Conversations can be extended to the topics of diversity and difference and the role that each must play in a multilingual and multicultural society that seeks to be democratic.

Winslow, V. (1997). *Follow the Leader*. New York: Delacorte Press.

Set in 1971 in North Carolina, this is the story of a family trying to make a difference. Mrs. Adams remembers segregation laws from her childhood and now votes only for "people who want to make things better for everybody." Mr. Adams hires subcontractors according to their bids and not to who they are; he refuses to join a segregated country club with "the most beautiful golf course this side of Myrtle Beach" even though it would help him with business contacts. Both Mr. and Mrs. Adams support desegregation of the local schools, even though this means that their daughter Amanda will be bused out of their neighborhood to a downtown school. Resistant at first, Amanda eventually comes to appreciate the teachers and students in her new school and realizes that the friend she missed so much at first was not the kind of friend she wanted to keep.

Follow the Leader invites conversations about racist attitudes that continue to lurk at or just below the surface in contemporary life. The book encourages adolescents to interrogate their often tacit acceptance of questionable peer-group ethics and to rethink their own beliefs. Another important conversation that might emerge from this book relates to how the burden of carrying out policy decisions often falls on people who do not make the policy in the first place. In this case, adult citizens make the decision to desegregate the public schools, but the onus of working through all the problems of the implementation of this order falls on the children and teachers. Because one group elects to "think globally" in voting for integration, another group has to "act locally" in terms of figuring out how to make integration work.

References

Alvermann, D.E., Moon, J.S., & Hagood, M.C. (1999). *Popular culture in the classroom: Teaching and researching critical media literacy*. Newark, DE: International Reading Association; Chicago: National Reading Conference.

Bigelow, W., Christensen, L., Karp, S., Miner, B., & Peterson, B. (1994). *Rethinking our classrooms: Teaching for equity and justice*. Milwaukee, WI: Rethinking Schools.

Bourdieu, P. (1991). *Language and symbolic power*. Cambridge, MA: Harvard University Press.

Buckingham, D. (1993). *Children talking television: The making of television literacy*. London: Routledge Falmer Press.

Buckingham, D., & Sefton-Green, J. (1995). *Cultural studies goes to school: Reading and teaching popular media*. London: Taylor & Francis.

Comber, B. (1992). Critical literacy: A selective review and discussion of recent literature. *South Australian Educational Leader, 3*(1), 1–10.

Comber, B. (2001). Critical literacies and local action: Teacher knowledge and a new research agenda. In B. Comber & A. Simpson (Eds.), *Negotiating critical literacies in classrooms* (pp. 271–282). Mahwah, NJ: Erlbaum.

Comber, B., & Simpson, A. (Eds.). (2001). *Negotiating critical literacies in classrooms*. Mahwah, NJ: Erlbaum.

Comber, B., & Thomson, P., with Wells, M. (2001). Critical literacy finds a "place": Writing and social action in a low-income Australian grade 2/3 classroom. *The Elementary School Journal, 101*(4), 451–464.

Edelsky, C. (Ed.). (2000). *Making justice our project*. Urbana, IL: National Council of Teachers of English.

Egawa, K., & Harste, J.C. (2001). What do we mean when we say we want our children to be literate? Balancing the literary curriculum: A new vision. *School Talk, 7*(1), 1–8.

Epstein, D. (1993). *Changing classroom cultures: Anti-racism, politics and schools*. Stoke-on-Trent, UK: Trentham Books.

Fehring, H., & Green, P. (Eds.). (2001). *Critical literacy: A collection of articles from the Australian Literacy Educators' Association*. Newark, DE: International Reading Association.

Fiske, J. (1989). *Reading the popular*. London: Routledge Press.

Flint, A.S., & Riordan-Karlsson, M. (2001). *Buried treasures in the classroom: Using hidden influences to enhance literacy teaching and learning*. Newark, DE: International Reading Association.

Galda, L., Rayburn, S., Stanzi, L.C. (2000). *Looking through the faraway end: Creating a literature-based reading curriculum with second graders*. Newark, DE: International Reading Association.

Granville, S. (1993). *Language, advertising, and power*. Johannesburg, South Africa: Witwatersrand University Press.

Harste, J.C. (1997, July). *Curriculum as audit trail: Underlying premises*. Paper presented at the Whole Language Umbrella Conference, Rochester, New York.

Harste, J.C. (2001, July). The Halliday Plus Model. Presentation given at the 2001 InterLERN workshop, Mississauga, ON.

Harste, J.C., Leland, C., Lewison, M., Ociepka, A., & Vasquez, V. (2000). Supporting critical conversations in classrooms. In K.M. Pierce (Ed.), *Adventuring with books* (pp. 507–512). Urbana, IL: National Council of Teachers of English.

Harste, J.C., & Vasquez, V. (1998). The work we do: Journal as audit trail. *Language Arts, 75*(4), 266–276.

Heffernan, L., & Lewison, M. (2000). Making real-world issues our business: Critical literacy in a third-grade classroom. *Primary Voices K–6, 9*(2), 15–21.

Janks, H. (1993). *Language identity and power*. Johannesburg, South Africa: Witwatersrand University Press.

Kavanagh, K. (1997). *Texts on television: School literacies through viewing in the first years of school*. Adelaide, South Australia: Department of Education and Children's Services.

Klein, N. (2000). *No logo: Taking aim at the brand name bullies*. Toronto: Vintage Canada Press.

Leland, C., Harste, J., Ociepka, A., Lewison, M., & Vasquez, V. (1999). Exploring critical literacy: You can hear a pin drop. *Language Arts, 77*(1), 70–77.

Luke, A., & Freebody, P. (1997). Shaping the social practices of reading. In S. Muspratt, A. Luke, & P. Freebody (Eds.), *Construction of critical literacies* (pp. 185–226). Cresskill, NJ: Hampton Press.

Luke, A., & Freebody, P. (1999). Further notes on the four resources model. *Reading Online*. Retrieved July 15, 2000, from http://www.readingonline.org/past/past_index.asp?HREF=../research/lukefreebody.html

Manning, A. (1993). Curriculum as conversation. In *Foundations of literacy*. Halifax, Nova Scotia: Mount Saint Vincent University.

Marsh, J. (2000). "But I want to fly too!": Girls and superhero play in the infant classroom. *Gender and Education, 12*(2), 209–220.

McLaren, P., Hammer, R., Sholle, D., Smith Reilly, S. (1995). *Rethinking media literacy: A critical pedagogy of representation*. New York: Peter Lang.

Mellor, B., O'Neill, M., & Patterson, A. (2000). *Reading stories: Activities and texts for critical readings*. Urbana, IL: National Council of Teachers of English.

Morgan, W. (1997). *Critical literacy in the classroom*. New York: Routledge Press.

Muspratt, S., Luke, A., & Freebody, P. (1997). *Constructing critical literacies: Teaching and learning textual practice.* Cresskill, NJ: Hampton Press.

Newfield, D. (1993). *Words and pictures.* Johannesberg, South Africa: Witwatersrand University Press.

O'Brien, J. (1994). Show Mum you love her: Taking a new look at junk mail. *Reading, 28*(1), 43–46.

Rudd, D. (1999). Fiction: Five run around together—Clearing a discursive space for children's literature. In I. Parker & the Bolton Discourse Network, *Critical textwork* (pp. 40–52). Philadelphia: Open University Press.

Rule, P. (1993). *Language and the news.* Johannesburg, South Africa: Witwatersrand University Press.

Schmidt, K. (1998, August). *Math investigations.* Presentation given at the 1998 InterLERN workshop, Mississauga, ON.

Short, K., Harste, J., & Burke, C. (1996). *Creating classrooms for authors and inquirers.* Portsmouth, NH: Heinemann.

Vasquez, V. (1998). Building equitable communities: Taking social action in a kindergarten classroom. *Talking Points, 9*(2), 3–6.

Vasquez, V. (1999). *Negotiating critical literacies with young children.* Unpublished doctoral dissertation, Indiana University, Bloomington, Indiana.

Vasquez, V. (2000). Building community through social action. *School Talk, 5*(4), 2–3.

Vasquez, V. (2000). Language stories and critical literacy lessons. *Talking Points, 11*(2), 5–7.

Vasquez, V. (2000). Our way: Using the everyday to create a critical literacy curriculum. *Primary Voices, 9*(2), 8–13.

Vasquez, V. (2001). *Creating a critical literacy curriculum with young children* (Phi Delta Kappa International Research Bulletin No. 29). Bloomington, IN: Phi Delta Kappa.

Vasquez, V. (2001). Negotiating critical literacies in elementary classrooms. In B. Comber & A. Simpson (Eds.), *Critical literacy at elementary sites.* Mahwah, NJ: Erlbaum.

Vasquez, V. (2003). *Using the everyday: Constructing critical literacies with young children.* Mahwah, NJ: Erlbaum.

Vasquez, V., & Egawa, K. (Eds.). (2002). Everyday texts, everyday literacies. *School Talk, 8*(1), 1–8.

Children's Book References

Bartoletti, S. (1999). *Kids on strike!* Boston: Houghton Mifflin.

Blumberg, R. (1996). *Bloomers.* New York: Aladdin.

Breckler, R. (1996). *Sweet dried apples: A Vietnamese wartime childhood.* Ill. D.K. Ray. Boston: Houghton Mifflin.

Browne, A. (1990). *Piggybook.* New York: Knopf.

Brumbeau, J. (2000). *The quilt maker's gift.* Ill. Gail de Marcken. New York: Scholastic.

Bunting, E. (1998). *So far from the sea.* Ill. C. Soentpiet. New York: Clarion Books.

Bunting, E. (1998). *Your move.* Ill. J. Ransome. New York: Harcourt Brace.

Childerhose, R.J. (1981). The hockey story. In C. Graves & C. McClymont (Eds.), *Contexts: Anthology one.* Scarborough, ON, Canada: Nelson Canada.

Clement, R. (1991). *Counting on Frank.* Milwaukee, WI: Gareth Stevens.

Coerr, E. (1979). *Sadako and the thousand paper cranes.* New York: Yearling.

Cole, B. (1997). *Princess Smartypants.* New York: Putnam.

Coleman, E. (1996). *White socks only.* Ill. T. Geter. Morton Grove, IL: Albert Whitman.

Cronin, D. (2000). *Click, clack, moo: Cows that type.* Ill. B. Lewin. New York: Simon & Schuster.

Dash, J. (1996). *We shall not be moved: The women's factory strike of 1909.* New York: Scholastic.

Fradin, D., & Fradin, J. (2001). *Ida B. Wells: Mother of the Civil Rights movement.* New York: Clarion Books.

Gac-Artigas, A. (2001). *Yo Alejandro* (2nd English ed.). Fairview, NJ: Ediciones Nuevo Espacio.

Hesse, K. (1996). *Music of dolphins.* New York: Scholastic.

Hinton, S.E. (1997). *The outsiders* (Reprint ed.). White Plains, NY: Prentice Hall.

Kaplan, W. (1998). *One more border: The true story of one family's escape from war-torn Europe.* Ill. S. Taylor. Toronto: Groundwood Books.

Lebert, B. (2001). *Crazy.* Vancouver, WA: Vintage International.

Lester, J. (1998). *From slave ship to freedom road.* New York: Puffin.

Loribiecki, M. (1996). *Just one flick of a finger.* Ill. D. Diaz. New York: Dial.

McCully, E.A. (1996). *The bobbin girl.* New York: Dial.

McCully, E.A. (1998). *The ballot box battle.* New York: Knopf.

McGuffee, M. (1997). *The day the earth was silent*. Bloomington, IN: Inquiring Voices Press.

Meyer, S.H., & Meyer, J. (Eds). (2001). *Teen ink: Friends and family*. Newton, MA: The Young Authors Foundation.

Miller, W. (1998). *The bus ride*. Ill. J. Ward. New York: Lee & Low.

Mochizuki, K. (1997). *Passage to freedom: The Sugihara story*. Ill. D. Lee. New York: Lee & Low.

Morrison, T., & Morrison, S. (1999). *The big box*. Burbank, CA: Disney Press.

Munsch, R. (1988). *The paper bag princess*. Toronto: Annick Press.

Perry, S. (1995). *If....* Oxford, UK: Oxford University Press Children's Books.

Ringgold, F. (1999). *If a bus could talk: The story of Rosa Parks*. New York: Simon & Schuster.

Shange, N. (1997). *White wash*. New York: Walker.

Tamaki, M. (2000). *Cover me*. Toronto: McGilligan Books.

Tetro, M. (1994). *The Royal Canadian Mounted Police*. St. Laurent, Quebec: Marc Tetro Canada.

Winslow, V. (1997). *Follow the leader*. New York: Delacorte Press.

Yamate, S. (1992). *Ashok by any other name*. Chicago: Polychrome Publications.

Index

Note: Page references followed by *b* or *f* indicate boxes or figures, respectively.